HIGHLIGHT
Intermediate
Workbook

Michael Vince

Heinemann International
A division of Heinemann Publishers (Oxford) Ltd
Halley Court, Jordan Hill, Oxford OX2 8EJ

OXFORD LONDON EDINBURGH
MADRID ATHENS BOLOGNA PARIS
MELBOURNE SYDNEY AUCKLAND SINGAPORE TOKYO
IBADAN NAIROBI HARARE GABORONE
PORTSMOUTH NH (USA)

ISBN 0 435 28634 X

© Michael Vince

First published 1992

All rights reserved; no part of this publication may be reproduced, stored in a retrieval system, or transmitted in any form or by any means, electronic, mechanical, photocopying, recording, or otherwise, without the prior written permission of the Publishers.

Designed by Ron Kamen
Illustrations by Phil Burrows, Chris Rothero and Willow.

Typeset by Gecko Limited, Bicester, Oxon
Printed and bound in Great Britain by
Alloa Printing and Publishing Co, Alloa.

91 92 93 94 95 96 97 10 9 8 7 6 5 4 3 2 1

Unit 1 The way we are

▶ Present simple
▶ Past simple

Present simple ▶ Student's Book p109

1   For each sentence **a** to **h** choose the most suitable ending **1** to **8**.

   a I usually get up . . .   4
   b Then I take a shower . . .   ___
   c At about a quarter to eight . . .   ___
   d I usually have to wait . . .   ___
   e I get to work . . .   ___
   f And occasionally I arrive late . . .   ___
   g I usually finish work at five . . .   ___
   h I sometimes go out in the evening . . .   ___

   1 . . . for at least ten minutes.
   2 . . . I leave and walk to the bus stop.
   3 . . . and I go home straight away.
   4 . . . at seven and make my own breakfast.
   5 . . . or sometimes I have a bath.
   6 . . . but usually I stay at home.
   7 . . . by half past eight if I'm lucky.
   8 . . . but it doesn't happen often.

Writing

2   Write a description of your own daily routine based on question 1.

   I usually get up _____
   _____
   _____
   _____
   _____

Past simple: question forming ▶ SB p109

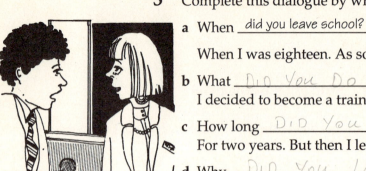

3 Complete this dialogue by writing the questions.

a When _did you leave school?_
When I was eighteen. As soon as I had taken my exams in fact.

b What _DID YOU DO THEN?_
I decided to become a trainee manager in a supermarket.

c How long _DID YOU WORK AS A TRAINE MANAGER_
For two years. But then I left.

d Why _DID YOU LEAVE_
I didn't find it very interesting, and I wanted a change.

e What _DID YOU THEN ?_
I work as a tourist guide, mainly in Britain, but also abroad.

Present simple and past simple

4 Complete the text by putting one of the verbs given into each space. Choose the best tense: present simple or past simple. Use each verb once only.

become   change   choose   decide   enjoy   find   know   like   love
meet   realise   tell   think   want   work

Many people who [1] _choose_ a career at an early age often [2] _REALISE_ later that they not [3] _DON'T LIKE_ their job. What should you do in this situation? Let's take Shirley Parks as an example. At the age of sixteen Shirley [4] _BECAME_ a nursery nurse. 'I [5] _KNEW_ something about this job, and I [6] _LOVED_ children, so I [7] _DECIDED_ it was the job for me,' she [8] _TOLD_ us. 'But after a year or so, I [9] _CHANGED_ that I [10] _WANTED_ a more demanding job. So I [11] _THOUGHT_ to join the police.' Now, five years later, Shirley [12] _WORKS_ in the centre of London in a busy police station. 'I [13] _LIKE_ my work. I am never bored. I [14] _MEET_ a lot of people every day, and my job [15] _CHANGES_ all the time.'

Vocabulary: go

5 Write *You can go* where possible beside each activity below.

You can go dancing	(Not Possible) listening to music
(not possible) playing chess	You can go shopping
(Not Possible) cooking	(Not Possible) playing football
You can go skating	You can go swimming
(Not Possible) eating	You can go camping
You can go jogging	You can go sailing

Vocabulary: word families and parts of speech

6 Use a dictionary to check the meaning of these words. Label each word **verb, noun, adjective** or **adverb**.

possible — adjective	encourage — VERB
possibly — ADVERB	encouragement — NOUN
possibility — NOUN	encouraged — PAST AND PAST-PARTICIPLE
impossible — ADJECTIVE	discourage — VERB (vt)
advice — NOUN	imagine — VERB
advise — VERB	imagination — NOUN
adviser — NOUN	imaginary — ADJECTIVE
advisable — ADJECTIVE	imaginative — ADJECTIVE

7 Use one of the words from question 6 to complete each sentence.

a I think you should take my ___advice___ and buy these trousers.

b There is a strong ___POSSIBILITY___ that we will have more of these shirts in stock next week.

c If you want to be a good fashion designer, you have to have some ___ADVICE___.

d I wanted to become a fashion model, but my parents ___DISCOURAGE___ me.

e When you choose a career, try to get your parents' ___ADVISE___.

f It's ___IMPOSSIBLE___ to dress well unless you have a lot of money!

g My best friend always ___ADVISE___ me about what clothes to wear.

h Her choice of clothes for the fancy-dress part was very ___IMAGINATIVE___.

3

Vocabulary: *make* or *do*?

8 Write **either** *you can make* or *you can do* before each word below.

<u>You can make</u> a joke.   <u>You can do</u> some homework.

<u>You can do</u> business.   <u>You can make</u> a noise.

<u>You can make</u> an offer.   <u>You can do</u> some housework.

<u>You can make</u> a choice.   <u>You can do</u> an exercise.

<u>You can make</u> a cake.   <u>You can make</u> a decision.

<u>You can make</u> a mistake.   <u>You can do</u> the shopping.

Skills: Reading and Listening ▶ SB p4

9 a Use a dictionary to check the differences between:

to wear   to dress   to put on

<u>Underline</u> examples of *wear* and *dress* in the text.

b Complete each sentence using either *wear*, *dress* or *put on* in a suitable form.

1 What did you <u>WEAR</u> to Helen's birthday party?

2 When I get up late I have to <u>DRESS</u> very quickly.

3 I like Jack's hairstyle, and I like the way he <u>DRESSES</u>.

4 Suddenly he stood up, <u>PUT ON</u> his coat, and left the room.

5 Michael always <u>WEARS</u> the same trousers and pullover!

c Find these words in the text:

annoys   to look   cost   second-hand   afford   fashionable   practical

Check their meanings in a dictionary if necessary.
Complete the sentences below.

1 It annoys me when people _____

2 I think people look good when they wear _____

3 Good quality clothes cost _____

4 It's not a good idea to buy a second-hand _____

5 I never _____ because I can't afford them.

6 This year _____ are very fashionable.

7 I like wearing _____ because they are very practical.

Writing

10 Imagine that you live in 2090. Write about the differences between your routine, and the way that people worked and lived in the distant past of the 1990s. Use these notes as a guide.

	NOW (2090)	IN THE PAST (1990)
Typical Day:	Robot brings breakfast (pills). Study, fly to watch robot football.	Get up early. Eat fruit, eggs. Take bus to work/school.
Sports:	Take exercise in computer gymnasium.	Go jogging, play tennis.
Work:	An hour a day. At home, using computers. Work for ten years then retire.	Seven hours a day. In offices, factories. Work for about 40 years.
Studying:	Astrophysics ASTROFIZIK telepathy (by computer).	Use books, write with pens. Forget things, take tests.
Other:	Live in space.	Live on Earth.

Complete the paragraphs, using the notes. Add your own ideas.

Nowadays, in the 21st century, we have computers and robots to help us and we don't have to work hard. So here is a description of what I have to do, and my normal routine. I usually wake up at about 8.00 and my robot brings me some pills for breakfast. _____

_____

_____

_____

_____

In the 1990s, however, life was very different. They used to do completely different things, and they had to do a lot of things which we find very strange. For example, people used to eat fruit or eggs for breakfast. _____

_____

_____

_____

_____

Pronunciation and listening

11 a 🔲 Listen and repeat these words.

foot feet fit fat   bet but bar bore
hot hoot hate height   bow bough beer bear

b 🔲 Listen and circle the word you hear.

feet/fit   hate/hat   bar/bore   hear/hair   beat/bite

c 🔲 Listen to this extract from SB Skills: Listening and Writing p8. In each space, write the word you hear.

Louise We also ___had to___ wear school uniform, we had to wear a brown ___skirt___ and a beige jumper and a cream ___shirt___ with a brown ___tie___. And it wasn't a very comfortable uniform to wear and it wasn't very ___attractive___ either, but we had to wear it, it was very strictly enforced. And they ___always___ made sure that we had ___hair___ _____ cut neatly and we didn't wear make-up or ___earrings___.

Vocabulary consolidation

12 Make lists of words you have learned in this unit under this heading:

Clothes and Fashion

Unit 2 Earning a living

▶ Present simple
▶ Present continuous

Present simple and present continuous ▶ SB p109

1 Put each verb in brackets into either the present simple or the present continuous.

I [1 work] ___work___ in a factory which [2 make] ___MAKES___ plastic pipes. I [3 not like] ___DON'T LIKE___ the job very much because I [4 do] ___DO___ the same things every day. I [5 want] ___WANT___ to find a new job but my friend Terry [6 tell] ___TELLING___ me that I should stay. He [7 look] ___LOOKING___ for a job but he can't find one, which is strange because they [8 build] ___ARE BUILDING___ a lot of new factories in our town. Of course, Terry [9 not dress] ___DOESN'T___ very well and he [10 usually arrive] ___ARRIVES___ late everywhere. He [11 train] ___IS TRAINING___ to be an accountant and he [12 go] ___GOES___ to college every day, but his parents [13 not send] ___DON'T SEND___ him any money. That's why he usually [14 come] ___COMES___ round to my house to eat. But luckily he's a good cook so at the moment while I [15 write] ___I'M WRITING___ this, he [16 cook] ___IS COOKING___ the dinner.

2 Match each question with the most suitable answer.

a Where are you living at the moment? ___5___

b What's happening outside, there's a lot of noise? ___4___

c How do you make this taste so nice? ___7___

d What's the score? I missed the first half. ___6___

e Hey, just a minute, what are you doing? ___3___

f What do you do? ___1___

g Are you having a good time? ___2___

1 I'm a police officer.

2 No, my boyfriend is dancing with somebody else.

3 I'm taking this television back to where it belongs.

4 The people opposite are having a party.

5 I'm staying in a hotel until I find a flat.

6 United are leading 2–0 at the moment.

7 You put some lemon in just before you serve it.

7

Vocabulary: jobs

3 Match each word in **A** with a job in **B**. More than one answer may be possible. Check meanings in a dictionary if necessary.

A animals   rubbish   pupils   buildings   tips
operations   cars   cheques   pipes   audiences
models   courts   patients   customers   money

B vet __animals__   surgeon __OPERATIONS__   shop assistant __CUSTOMER__
accountant __Cheques__   lawyer __COURTS__   waiter __TIPS__
mechanic __CAR__   actor __AUDIENCES__   photographer __MODELS__
nurse __PATIENTS__   teacher __PUPIPILS__   plumber __PIPES__
architect __BUILDINGS__   bank clerk __CHEQUES__   dustman __RUBBISH__

4 Match each sentence with a job from the list in question 3B. More than one answer may be possible.

a You have to be good at dealing with worried owners. __vet__
b You have to wear special clothes because you will get dirty. __Dustman__
c You have to know a lot about engines. __Mechanic__
d You have to look carefully at the light. __PHOTOGRAPHER__
e You could get wet in this job. __PLUMBER__
f You have to be good at making ill people feel comfortable. __NURSE__
g You have to be polite and work fast if you want extra money. __WAITER__
h You have to be good at saving money for your customers. __ACCOUNTANT__

5 Put one word from the list into each space.

deal   employer   involve   paid   polite   punctual   staff   training

Do you have a job, or are you still thinking about a career? Jobs vary a great deal, and very few are exactly the same. [1] __Training__ may be necessary, and the job may [2] __involve__ technical knowledge of some kind. Different companies also expect different things from their [3] __Staff__. For example, you may have to [4] __Deal__ with only routine matters at first. If you have to talk to customers, then you are expected to be [5] __Polite__, and your [6] __employer__ will certainly expect you to be [7] __Punctual__. Finally, remember that even if your job is not well [8] __Paid__, you should always act responsibly.

Understanding text: jobs

6 Read the text and complete the statements that follow.

> I enjoy my job, even though it is quite difficult and I have a lot of different duties. I welcome the guests and make them feel at home, but I don't **actually** show them to their rooms – that's the porter's job. I also answer their enquiries and give them information about railway timetables **and that kind of thing**, or general tourist information. The worst part of my job is **that I do nights for one week in every month**. There isn't much work then, but I **don't** like doing it. The other thing I don't like is that sometimes guests **make complaints** or are a bit rude. I try to be polite but it can be difficult. **But on the whole** it's an interesting job. I had to do a training course in hotel management, and if I do well in the job it's possible for me to **become a manager** one day. Or maybe even have my own hotel.

a In my job I have to _welcome the guests_
    and I also have to _MAKE THEM FEEL AT HOME_

b I don't have to _SHOW THEM TO THEIR ROOMS_

c In general I like my job because _I HAVE A LOT OF DIFFERENT DUTIES_,
    though I don't like _I DO NIGHTS FOR ONE WEEK IN EVER MONTH_
    and feel annoyed when _SOMETIMES GUEST MAKE COMPLAINTS OR ARE A BIT Rude._

d It's important in this job to be _AN HOTEL MANAGER._

e To get a job like this you need _TO HAVE A LOT OF DIFFERENT DUTIES & POLITENESS_

f There are quite good prospects in the job: I could _BECOME ON MANAGER ONE DAY_ or _MAYBE EVEN HAVE MY OWN HOTEL._

Vocabulary: personal qualities for jobs

7 Use a dictionary to check the meaning of the words below. Complete the lists by adding the missing forms of the words.

Noun	Adjective	Noun	Adjective
experience	experienced	organisation	_____
enthusiasm	_____	_____	reliable
versatility	_____	_____	patient
_____	confident	_____	honest
_____	responsible	independence	_____

8 Use one of the words from question 7 in each sentence.

a You must show your _enthusiasm_ for your job by seeming interested.

b Any job involving money means that you must be very _____ .

c Most employers prefer staff who can work alone and be _____ .

d It's no good being untidy and in a mess. You have to be _____ .

e If you have _____ , then you believe that you will succeed.

f Being _____ , showing that you can do different jobs, is important.

g You have to do what you promise, or people will not think you _____ .

h Dealing with customers who may be rude, requires a lot of _____ .

Likes, dislikes and abilities ▶ SB p115

9 Complete each statement in a suitable way.

a In my job, you have to be good at _____

b I am successful in my job, partly because I know how to _____
_____

c In my job, I really enjoy _____

d I don't mind _____
but I can't stand _____

Writing using cues

10 Use these notes to write sentences about the person and the job. The verbs underlined must be put into the most suitable tense form.
Add other words where necessary.

a <u>Go</u> school/Bradford/<u>leave</u>/school/1987.

   She went to school in Bradford and she left school in 1987.

b At the moment Nancy Hills/<u>work</u>/assistant manager/large department store/centre/Bradford.

c She <u>start</u>/working there/1989.

d Before that/<u>work</u>/typist.

e Now/<u>work</u> toy department/but last year/<u>work</u>/children's clothes department.

_____

f She <u>have</u> to serve/customers/but also/<u>learn</u>/<u>be</u>/manager.

_____

g Last month/<u>go</u>/London/<u>do</u>/training course and <u>learn</u>/<u>use</u>/computer.

_____

h She not <u>like</u>/<u>be</u> typist/because/<u>be</u>/no responsibility.

_____

One Make-Up Artist's Day ▶ SB p13: further activities

11 a Find these words and phrases in the text. Check their meanings in a dictionary if necessary.

by accident   got in touch with   instead   it sounds like   the sort
do all the hair   to gossip   portraits   to look forward to   living

b Rewrite each sentence, using one of the words or phrases from the list to replace the underlined part. Verbs may be used in different tenses and forms.

1 What <u>sort of job do you have</u>?

   What _do you do for a living?_

2 <u>I think this is probably</u> a good job.

   This _____ a good job.

3 She has painted a lot of <u>pictures of people</u>.

   She has painted a lot of _____

4 Do you <u>cut and set</u> your own hair?

   Do you _____ your own hair?

5 I met her <u>by chance</u>.

   I met her _____

6 I don't like the way he <u>talks about other people</u>.

   I don't like the way he _____

7 I planned to go out yesterday, but <u>in place of that</u> I stayed in.

   I planned to go out yesterday, But I stayed in _____

_____

8 I <u>expect to enjoy</u> my holiday in the summer.

I'm _____ my holiday in the summer.

9 Don't forget to <u>write or phone</u> the personnel manager.

Don't forget to _____ the personnel manager.

10 What <u>kind</u> of job do you want?

What _____ of job do you want?

Pronunciation and listening

12 a ☐ Listen and repeat these sentences.

1 They asked me to do it.	5 I stayed in all evening.
2 I decided to go there.	6 We washed the clothes.
3 She helped me to find it.	7 They allowed her to leave.
4 I worked in a bank.	8 He cleaned the windows.

b ☐ Listen to this extract from Skills: Listening and Writing SB p17, activity 4. In each space, write the word you hear.

Interviewer: And do you do the same things all the time?

Janet: _____ _____ _____ , yes I do, it's very much the same things all the time, but we change around, and I could go to a different department soon _____ _____ . It _____ _____ .

Interviewer: What about the daily routine? Do you have one?

Janet: Oh yes, _____ . The main thing I do first is I check the till.

Interviewer: That's the drawer with the money in it.

Janet: Yes, _____ _____ .

Vocabulary consolidation

13 Make lists of words you have learned in this unit under these headings.

Work: personal qualities   **Work: conditions**

Progress Test 1

Units 1 and 2

1 Choose the most suitable answer for each question. Circle the number.

a What did you enjoy most when you were on holiday?

1 To go sailing.
2 To sail.
3 Going sailing.
4 Going to sail.

b What do you usually do at the weekend?

1 I go to the cinema.
2 I am going to the cinema.
3 I used to go to the cinema.
4 I am usually to the cinema.

c Do you like sport?

1 I am not interesting in it.
2 I don't interest in it.
3 I don't interested in it.
4 I am not interested in it.

d Is your new job very difficult?

1 No, I musn't work very hard.
2 No, I don't have to work very hard.
3 No, I am not allowed to work very hard.
4 No, I haven't to work very hard.

e Does your brother like his new job?

1 He can't stand to get up early.
2 He doesn't stand getting up early.
3 He can't stand getting up early.
4 He stands getting up early.

f What do you have for lunch?

1 I am usually having a sandwich.
2 I usually am having a sandwich.
3 I have usually a sandwich.
4 I usually have a sandwich.

g What's the most important part of your job?

1 I have to be good to deal with people.
2 I have to be good at dealing with people.
3 I have to be good with dealing with people.
4 I have to be good dealing with people.

h Why don't you use the computer?

1 I don't know to use it.
2 I don't know using it.
3 I don't know how to use it.
4 I don't know use it.

13

i What happened in the lesson on Monday?

   1 We are having a test.   **3** We used to have a test.
   2 We have a test.   **4** We had a test.

j What do you do?

   1 I work as a lawyer.   **3** I work a lawyer.
   2 I am lawyer.   **4** I do a lawyer.

10 marks

2 Put each verb in brackets into a suitable tense and form.

   a Where (you eat) _____ last night? (You go) _____ to the new Chinese restaurant?

   b Your job must be interesting. What (you do) _____ exactly?

   c He (fall) _____ down the stairs yesterday and (have) _____ to go to hospital.

   d I (not want) _____ to go for a walk now. It (rain) _____ .

   e (Sue like) _____ playing basketball?

   f Where you usually (stay) _____ when you (go) _____ to Hamburg?

   g (you understand usually) _____ everything she (tell) _____ you?

   h What you (do) _____ after last night's match?

   i Mr Smith (be) _____ free a few minutes ago, but now he (talk) _____ to some customers.

15 marks

3 Make each sentence into a question.

   a Philip works in an electronics factory.

   _____

   b They had to write their homework again.

   _____

   c Julie often has to work at weekends.

   _____

   d Richard's waiting for us downstairs.

   _____

   e They lost their suitcases at the airport.

   _____

f You're reading my newspaper.

_____

g Janet likes fish and chips.

_____

h Helen knew all the answers.

_____

i They usually stay at the Grand Hotel.

_____

j Sally left this morning.

_____

10 marks

4 Put one suitable word in each space.

Andrew [1] _____ school when he was sixteen, and found a [2] _____ as a trainee manager in a supermarket. He [3] _____ to work hard but he enjoyed it. [4] _____ morning he arrived at work at seven thirty and he never left until after six in the evening. He did the [5] _____ kinds of things at [6] _____ , but soon the job became more interesting. He had to [7] _____ with all the orders for new products and [8] _____ the cash to the bank every afternoon. The job was not very well [9] _____ , but he learned a lot. Now he is the manager of a large supermarket, and [10] _____ most of his time sitting in his office.

10 marks

Unit 3 It couldn't happen to me

▶ Past simple
▶ Past continuous

Past simple and past continuous ▶ SB p109

1 These sentences make one continuous story. Put each verb in brackets into the most suitable past tense.

a One Sunday while I [make] *was making* my breakfast I [hear] *heard* a knock at the door.

b I [put on] _____ my dressing-gown and [go] _____ to open it.

c My neighbour [look for] _____ his cat and [want] _____ me to help him find it.

d I [explain] _____ that I [have] _____ breakfast.

e Unfortunately I [forget] _____ my breakfast which still [cook] _____ .

f I [burn] _____ my eggs and bacon and the kitchen filled with smoke.

g When I [open] _____ the window to let out the smoke I [see] _____ the cat.

h It [sit] _____ at the top of a tree and it [try] _____ to get down.

i I [put] _____ my burned breakfast into a dish and [leave] _____ it outside the door.

j As soon as the cat [smell] _____ the food, it [jump] _____ down from the tree.

Present simple, past simple, past continuous ▶ SB p109

2 Put each verb in the text into one of the following tenses: present simple, past simple, past continuous.

I have a very bad memory, and a few years ago something very silly [1 happen] _happened_ to me while I [2 travel] _____ home from my office in London. I [3 sit] _____ on the train as usual, when I [4 realise] _____ that I [5 not have] _____ my briefcase with me. I had left it behind at the station! So, very unhappily, I [6 get out] _____ at the next station, and [7 take] _____ a train back to London. However, even after searching everywhere I [8 not find] _____ my case at the station. In the end, I [9 go] _____ home, and the next day I [10 buy] _____ a new briefcase before I [11 arrive] _____ at work. Unfortunately, the missing briefcase [12 contain] _____ some important papers, so my boss [13 make] _____ me work late for a week. On Friday night, while I [14 put] _____ my things away I [15 notice] _____ something on the floor under the desk. It was the missing briefcase, of course. I [16 not know] _____ whether to laugh or cry!

Time expressions ▶ SB p119

3 Put one time expression from the list into each space. Some words may be used more than once.

then   when   while   in the end

[a] __When__ the alarm clock went off, Penny jumped out of bed. It was dark outside and very cold. She quickly washed and [b] _____ tried to decide what to wear. [c] _____ she had to put on the first warm clothes she could find and run for the bus. [d] _____ she was half way to the stop, the bus came past. 'Oh no,' she thought, 'I'm going to be late'. However, [e] _____ she was waiting for the next bus, a car stopped in front of her, and [f] _____ she looked up, she realised that the driver was Greg Edwards, 'Can I give you a lift?' he asked. Penny couldn't believe her luck, and she opened the door and got in.

17

Writing

4 Continue the story in question 3, starting as shown. Use the pictures as a guide.

While they were driving through the town centre _____
_____
_____
_____
_____
_____

Past simple and past continuous: questions and answers

5 Match each question with the most suitable answer. More than one answer may be possible.

a What was she doing when I phoned her last night. ___6___

b What did she do when she left school? _____

c When did she realise that her wallet was missing? _____

d What did she do when the car broke down? _____

e What was she doing when you first met her? _____

f What did she do after she paid the bill? _____

g What was she saying when you asked her about it? _____

h What was she doing when you stopped to give her a lift? _____

1 She was working as an assistant in a clothes shop.

2 She walked to the nearest bus stop.

3 A few minutes after she left the restaurant.

4 She was watching a rather silly film on television.

5 She was walking to the bus stop.

6 She was talking about her new records.

7 She realised that the bill included three drinks too many!

8 She found a job as an assistant in a clothes shop.

Past simple and past continuous: completion dialogue

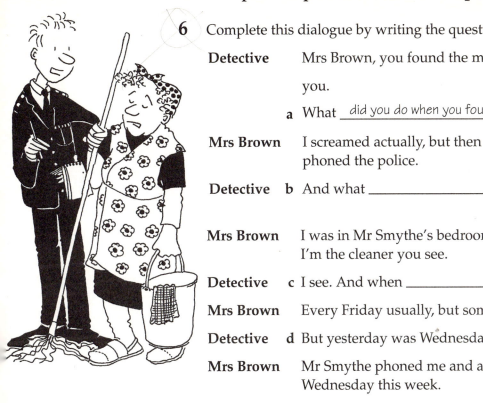

6 Complete this dialogue by writing the questions.

Detective   Mrs Brown, you found the murdered man's body, didn't you.
   a What _did you do when you found it?_____

Mrs Brown   I screamed actually, but then I pulled myself together and I phoned the police.

Detective   **b** And what _____

Mrs Brown   I was in Mr Smythe's bedroom because I was cleaning it. I'm the cleaner you see.

Detective   **c** I see. And when _____

Mrs Brown   Every Friday usually, but sometimes I clean it on Monday.

Detective   **d** But yesterday was Wednesday. Why _____

Mrs Brown   Mr Smythe phoned me and asked me to clean the house on Wednesday this week.

Detective   **e** Why _____

Mrs Brown   I don't know. I didn't ask him. And now it's too late.

Likes, dislikes and ability ▶ SB p115

7 Complete each sentence with a suitable ending beginning with either an *-ing* form, an infinitive **with** *to*, or an infinitive **without** *to*. Choose the endings from this list:

to try something different   meeting interesting people   try to enjoy it
to deal with angry customers   to travel more   working at night
sitting indoors all the time   making everything sound interesting

a Working in the music business is great and I really like _meeting_
   _interesting people._____

b I quite like this job but I really want _____

c It's an interesting job I suppose, but I'd like _____

d I don't mind wearing a uniform, but I hate _____

e It's not a difficult job, but you have to know how _____

f Success as a tour guide depends on your being good at _____

g Work in an office? No thanks! I really can't stand _____

h Don't complain so much about your job. You must _____

Prepositions of place and movement ▶ SB p120

8 Put one of the prepositions in the list into each space.

at   from   in   into   on   out   to

a Last night I went ____to____ the cinema with some friends.

b I met them _____ the bus stop _____ the end of the street.

c When I was _____ the bus I left my umbrella _____ the seat.

d The train _____ London arrived _____ Oxford station an hour late.

e When I arrived _____ Oxford I walked _____ the station and found a taxi.

f Janet came _____ the room and sat _____ one of the desks _____ the back.

g Last summer I cycled _____ Brighton _____ Eastbourne.

h You'll find the flowers _____ the table _____ the living room.

Orders, instructions and requests ▶ SB p115

9 Choose the most suitable expression from the words underlined.

a You <u>will go/go</u> along this street as far as the traffic lights and then you <u>turn/are turning</u> left.

b <u>Do you want/Shall I help you</u> do the ironing?

c <u>Feed the dog/You will feed the dog</u> before you go to school, please.

d <u>Do you think I could give you/Shall I give you</u> some help?

e Don't worry, <u>I'll cook the lunch/could I cook the lunch</u>?

f <u>Could I borrow/Shall I borrow</u> your car?

Skills: Reading and Listening ▶ SB p22: further activities

10 a Find these verbs in the text. Check their meanings in a dictionary.

survive   turn into   run out of   rescue   make a trip   land   wave   protect   raise the alarm   last

b Complete the text on page 21 by using the verbs from **a** in a suitable tense and form. Use each verb once. Note that not all the verbs are used.

Last summer I decided to [1] _____ to a small village in the mountains for a holiday. My trip started well enough, but it soon [2] _____ a nightmare. I got completely lost, and my car [3] _____ of petrol in the middle of nowhere. So I decided to take a short cut by continuing on foot across the mountains, but I fell and hurt my leg. I [4] _____ at some people on the road below, but they didn't take any notice, and then it started snowing. I [5] _____ myself from the cold by making a shelter from branches. I lit a fire and waited for someone to [6] _____ me. Luckily some hunters saw the smoke and [7] _____ . A few hours later a helicopter [8] _____ nearby, and I was taken to hospital.

Pronunciation and listening

11 a Listen and repeat the words from the list.

pack/back   tin/thin   win/wing   log/lock
van/fan   those/doze   sock/shock   rice/rise

b Listen again and (circle) the word you hear.

c Listen to this extract from Skills: Listening and Writing SB p26. In each space, write the word you hear.

Roger Got it. But just remind me again who I'm going to see.

Ann _____ _____ Mr Stubbs. His office is on the second floor. Give him the packet and he'll give you an envelope in exchange. _____ _____ _____ . Then you bring the envelope back here.

Roger Are you sure this is all right Ann? There's nothing, _____ _____ , wrong about all this, _____ _____ . It does seem a bit fishy to me.

Ann Roger, _____ _____ _____ . You know you can trust me, don't you? Now, just listen carefully and I'll _____ _____ the directions again.

Vocabulary consolidation

12 Make a list of words you have learned in this unit under this heading:

Verbs in their past tense form

Unit 4 It's a bargain

▶ Future time
▶ Prepositions of movement, position and time

Future time ▶ SB p111

1 Put each verb in brackets into *going to*, future use of present continuous or present simple.

   a (you do) <u>Are you doing</u> anything on Friday? We could go to the cinema.

   b Look at that plane flying so low! I think it (crash) _____ .

   c Thursday is a holiday, so I'm (sleep) _____ all morning.

   d Here are your tickets. The show (start) _____ at 7.30.

   e What a goal! I think that City (win) _____ this game.

   f I don't know what to buy my sister for Christmas. What you (give) _____ her?

   g Could you check my diary and tell me who I (meet) _____ on Monday?

   h Hurry up! The train (leave) _____ in five minutes.

Future time: question forms

2 Write a question for each answer.

   a Where <u>are you going on holiday this year?</u>
   To a Greek island I think, probably in July.

   b What _____
   A friend of mine has got some tickets for the new play at the National Theatre.

   c What _____
   At 9.45. So try to be at the airport at about 8.30.

   d What _____
   Probably go to university, but I might get a job instead.

   e Why _____
   The bus is cheaper, and I'll get there much quicker.

Prepositions of movement, position and time ▶ SB p119, 120

3 Put one preposition from the list into each space.

at by from in on opposite to

a The shops open _from_ 9.00 _to_ 14.00, and open again _in_ the evening.

b Smoking is not allowed _____ the food hall or _____ the first floor.

c Please pay _____ the cash desk. Please put goods _____ the wire basket.

d This lift stops _____ each floor. The express lift is _____ .

e _____ Wednesday and Friday this shop closes _____ 20.30.

f Come _____ our bargain sale which starts _____ January 15th _____ 9.00.

g Please leave your shopping bags _____ the desk _____ the main entrance.

h Store detectives operate _____ this store.

Shopping: dialogue completion

4 Complete this dialogue.

Customer	Excuse me, _how much is this dress?_
Assistant	It's £12.50. And there's this one which is £9.00.
Customer	Which _____
Assistant	It's hard to say really. This one is cheaper of course but it's very good quality. It depends which colour you like.
Customer	Have _____
Assistant	That's the largest size I'm afraid. But we might have some more next week.
Customer	But I won't be here next week I _____
Assistant	Tomorrow? Are you? I didn't realise you were Italian. Perhaps you could buy a skirt instead. How _____
Customer	Yes, I like the colour. Can _____
Assistant	Yes, of course. The changing room is over there.

23

Decisions, suggestions, offers, arrangements, requests
▶ SB p114, 115

5 Complete the mini-dialogues by following the instructions.

a A Well, which one do you want, the green one or the blue one?
B (Decide to take the blue one)

  I'll take the blue one.

b A I really don't know what to buy Sue for Christmas.
B (Suggest a diary)

c A Gosh, I feel really hungry.
B (Offer to make a sandwich)

d A We could go out to lunch on Sunday.
B (Explain your arrangements – visit/grandmother)

e A Are you feeling hot?
B (Politely request to open the window)

Making comparisons with adjectives

6 Make a comparison between the items given.

a Fresh vegetables/frozen vegetables (tasty)

  Fresh vegetables are tastier than frozen vegetables.

b Meat/fish (expensive)

c Tinned milk/fresh milk (convenient)

d Fresh food/frozen food (healthy)

e Fast food/health food (fattening)

f Imported fruit/home-grown fruit (good)

Mixed tenses

7 Complete the text by putting one of the verbs into each space. Choose the most suitable tense and form. Use each verb once only.

be call come decide find go happen keep know miss need phone take tell understand

Dear Carol,

It was good to see you at the weekend. This is just a quick letter to tell you what [1] _happened_ after you [2] _____ home on Saturday. Ron and I finally [3] _____ to buy a motorbike and we [4] _____ one advertised in the local paper. We [5] _____ a way of getting to college, because at the moment we [6] _____ the bus every morning and you [7] _____ what the buses are like. We usually [8] _____ the first half an hour of lectures, and our tutor [9] _____ complaining. We [10] _____ about the bike, and the owner [11] _____ away on business, but his sister [12] _____ us to go round and see it this week. He is [13] _____ back on Saturday.

Could you come with us? You probably [14] _____ more about bikes than we do, so you can give us some advice. We [15] _____ at your place on Saturday morning at about 10.00.

　　See you then,

　　　Denise

Vocabulary: food

8 Study this list of words and divide them into five groups using the categories given. Check meanings in a dictionary if necessary.

chops	cheese	onions	beans	cakes
apples	bread	grapes	biscuits	cream
yoghurt	cabbage	peaches	pears	chicken
sausages	milk	carrots	steak	rolls

Vegetables	**Fruit**	**Dairy Products**	**Meat**	**Bakery Products**
cabbage	_____	_____	_____	_____
_____	_____	_____	_____	_____
_____	_____	_____	_____	_____
_____	_____	_____	_____	_____

25

9 Choose words from the list in question 8 which are:

   a Five things that you could eat for breakfast.
   _____

   b Five things you could eat cooked or uncooked.
   _____

   c Two things you like and two things you dislike.
   _____

   d Five pairs of things you could eat together.
   _____

   e A group of things which make a good meal.
   _____

Writing

10 Imagine that a rich relative has given you £1000 as a present for doing well in your English lessons. Write about how you are going to spend the money. This could be a description of what you are going to buy, or other things you are going to spend the money on (a holiday for example).

_____
_____
_____
_____
_____
_____
_____
_____
_____
_____
_____
_____
_____

Pronunciation and listening

11 a 🔲 Listen and repeat these sentences.

1 Small corner shops are much more expensive than supermarkets.
2 What are you doing tonight after the lesson?
3 Excuse me, do you know the way to the bus station?
4 I'm looking for a pub called 'The Coach and Horses'.
5 I'll come round and (pick you up) at half past seven.

b 🔲 Listen again and (circle) the syllables that have most stress.

c 🔲 Listen to the extract from Skills: Listening and Writing SB p35, activity 4. In each space, write the words you hear.

Assistant This is our ___Most Popular___ model. It's light, very

strong, and _____ _____ .

Ricky I had _____ _____ _____ , and I didn't

think it was very safe. I burnt myself once.

Jean _____ _____ _____ _____ safer?

Assistant Um . . . some people prefer gas. But the advantage with this

one is that you can _____ _____ _____

_____ _____ in a strong wind, or if it's raining.

Vocabulary consolidation

12 Make lists of words you have learned in this unit under this heading:

Shops and Shopping

Unit 5 On the road

▶ Past simple
▶ Present perfect simple
▶ Time expressions

Time expressions ▶ SB p119

1 Choose the most suitable expression from the words underlined.

a I've been working for this company (for)/since two years.

b I came here on holiday before three years ago.

c Thanks for the offer, but I've eaten an hour ago/already.

d Actually I've been to Crete four years ago/before.

e Already/lately I've been feeling very tired.

f She hasn't finished her dinner already/yet, I'm afraid.

g I think I saw Sue's cousin outside lately/a moment ago.

h Have you ever/yet been to that disco near the harbour?

2 Complete the text by putting one of the time expressions into each space. Use each one at least once. Some can be used several times.

ago   since   for many years   when   recently   very often
two weeks ago   for ages

I think bicycles are great! In fact, I've been riding a bicycle safely [1] _for many years_ , but [2] _____ I had a silly accident. It happened about [3] _____ . I went off the road and hit a tree and broke my arm and [4] _____ then I haven't been able to ride, of course. So I shall have to take a bus [5] _____ I go to work. I'm not looking forward to this, as I really hate it! Actually, I gave up buses about five years [6] _____ [7] _____ I started cycling everywhere. [8] _____ that time I have very rarely been ill, and I am much slimmer than I was. If you have been trying to lose weight [9] _____ , why not try cycling? You might end up with a broken arm like me, but that kind of thing doesn't happen [10] _____ . At least, not if you are careful!

28

Present perfect simple and past simple ▶ SB p109, 110

3 Put each verb in brackets into either present perfect simple or past simple.

a (he go) _Did he go_ to the supermarket when you asked him?

b How long you (know) _____ that this is Graham's car?

c I (not drive) _____ a car for the last three years.

d They told me to report to the police station but I (not go) _____ yet.

e I (ask) _____ her to help me yesterday, but she (refuse) _____ .

f She (start) _____ riding a motorbike six months ago.

g Mrs Lamb is 74 and she never (have) _____ an accident.

h What (you do) _____ when the car (break down) _____ ?

Giving directions

4 Complete the text by putting **one** suitable word into each space.

As you've never been to our house before, I thought I'd write and give you some [1] _directions_ how to get there. [2] _____ off the motorway where the signs say 'Sittingbourne'. Keep going for about ten miles and you come [3] _____ a main road. Turn right here and [4] _____ the road to Dover. It [5] _____ you to our village. When you reach the village, you come to a [6] _____ junction at the top of a hill. Turn right, and carry [7] _____ on until you see a church [8] _____ the right. There's a road [9] _____ the church. Go down that road and our house is [10] _____ the end of the road. You can't miss it.

Writing

5 Study this map which gives you directions to get to the house marked on the map. Use the map to complete directions for someone who is coming from London by car.

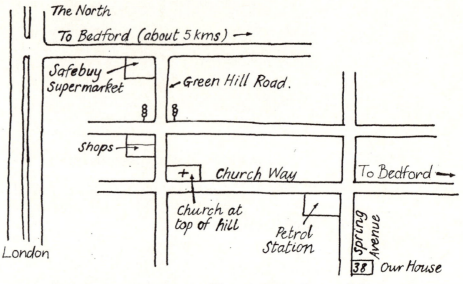

This is how to get to our house. It's quite easy. Turn off the motorway when you see a sign that says 'Bedford'. _____

_____
_____
_____
_____
_____

Mini-dialogues

6 Complete the mini-dialogues by following the instructions.

  a A What have you been doing lately?
   B (study, for exams)

   I've been studying for my exams.

  b A Would you like some lunch?
   B (no thanks, have lunch already)

   _____

  c A Have you ever been to London?
   B (yes, go there 1989)

   _____

d A Could you give me back that book you borrowed?
   B (sorry, not finish)
   _____

e A Have you met Keith?
   B (yes, meet at party last year)
   _____

f A Do you know Keith's brother?
   B (yes, know him since we be at school together)
   _____

g A Why is the floor so wet?
   B (just have a bath)
   _____

h A Could I speak to David, please?
   B (sorry, just leave)
   _____

Tense contrasts

7   Put each verb in brackets into either present simple, present continuous, past simple, past continuous, present perfect simple, or *will* and *going to*.

Last week while I [1 cycle] *was cycling* to work I [2 have] _____ an accident and all because of the weather! It [3 rain] _____ and there were a lot of wet leaves on the road. My bike [4 slip] _____ on the wet road, and I [5 fall] _____ off. Luckily a passing motorist [6 stop] _____ to help me. '[7 you hurt] _____ yourself?' she asked me. 'I think I [8 broke] _____ my arm,' I told her. '[9 not worry] _____ ', she said, 'I [10 take] _____ you to hospital.' At the hospital they [11 give] _____ me an X-ray and [12 ask] _____ me a lot of questions. '[13 you eat] _____ anything today?' a nurse asked me. 'What [14 you mean] _____?' I said. '[15 you have] _____ any breakfast before you [16 leave] _____ home?' she said. 'Why?' I said, feeling worried, '[17 I have] _____ an operation?' 'Of course not,' said the nurse. 'I [18 just make] _____ some tea. Would you like a cup?'

Skills: Reading and Listening ▶ **SB p40: further activities**

8 a Find these words and phrases in the text. Check their meanings in a dictionary if necessary.

brand new   save on   impressed   luxurious   it's not worth much
in lovely condition

b Rewrite this text, **so that it has the opposite meaning**, using the words and phrases in **a** instead of the phrases underlined.

Recently I bought <u>a second-hand car</u>. It was <u>in a shocking state</u>, and very <u>dirty and uncomfortable</u>. People told me I would <u>waste a lot</u> of money on petrol, and they were <u>not enthusiastic</u>. I showed it to a friend of mine, who is a mechanic. He disagreed. '<u>This is very valuable</u>,' he said, 'why don't you let me put in a new engine? I felt very confused!

Recently I bought a brand new car _____

_____

_____

_____

_____

_____

_____

_____

_____

Pronunciation and listening

9 a 🔲 Listen and repeat these words.

worries   money   done   lovely   decided   impressed
dealer   order   cloth   worth   reliable   economical

b 🔲 Listen to the extract from Skills: Reading and Listening SB p41, activity 5. In each space, write the word you hear.

Lynn I would say it costs me about £5 or £6 a week. (*Yes*) Sometimes I get a Travelcard, which you can use on the tube or on the buses, and _____ _____ _____ the bus. It depends how organised I'm feeling that week. _____ _____ _____ to use public transport, it's much cheaper than a car, and there's _____ _____ _____ , you can get anywhere quickly, especially on the Underground. While in a car you get stuck in a traffic jam.

Interviewer So you wouldn't consider running even a small car?

Lynn _____ _____ _____ _____ _____ for me. The big problem is parking (*well yes*) – there's simply nowhere to put it _____ _____ _____ _____ the centre, unless you feel like paying a fortune in a car-park.

Vocabulary consolidation

10 Make lists of words you have learned in this unit under these headings:

Parts of a Car   On the Road

Unit 6 Looking forward

▶ Articles
▶ Future time
▶ Countables and uncountables
▶ Conditional I

Articles ▶ SB p118

1 Complete each sentence with *a/an*, *the*, or by leaving the space.

a He's ____an____ engineer but he hasn't got ____a____ job at ____the____ moment.

b In _____ Scotland _____ many men wear _____ kilts.

c _____ judge sent him to _____ prison for _____ life.

d I don't really like _____ fish but I love _____ shellfish.

e His _____ father gives him _____ money every _____ Friday.

f Can you give me _____ information about _____ train to _____ Leeds?

g Go down _____ Bridge Street and you'll see _____ hospital on _____ right.

h I went on _____ guided tour to _____ United States.

Future time ▶ SB p111

2 Put the verb in brackets in each sentence into either *going to*, *will*, present continuous future use, or future continuous.

a She (have) __is having_____ a party on Friday.

b Life (be) _____ different in the 21st century.

c I expect she (live) _____ somewhere else next year.

d Look out! You (drop) _____ the teapot.

e Sorry, I can't. I (fly) _____ to Glasgow that morning.

f I hope (be) _____ famous soon!

g Oh no, it's broken! What (we use) _____ now?

h This one suits me I think. I (take) _____ it.

Future time clauses ▶ SB p112

3 Put each verb in brackets into either present simple or *will* form.

a Don't worry about your washing. The moment it (start) __starts__ to rain, I (take) __will take__ it in.

b When Jean (come) _____ home, I (tell) _____ her the news.

c I (wait) _____ here until Alex (phone) _____ .

d Before Nigel (leave) _____ I (give) _____ him the parcel.

e Never mind. We (change) _____ seats when the lights (come) _____ on.

f I (pay) _____ you as soon as I (get) _____ some money.

Too much, too many or *not enough* ▶ SB p118

4 Complete the comment on each situation using either *too much, too many* or *not enough*.

a You arrive at the airport with ten suitcases. At the check-in desk they look at your luggage and say:

Sorry, but you __'ve got too much luggage.__

b You are in the supermarket. At the cash desk, you look in your wallet and receive a shock. You say:

Sorry, but I _____

c You move from a small house to a large one. After putting all your furniture into the large house, it still seems empty. You say to your family:

Oh dear, we _____

d You go to a football match with a friend and there is a lot of fighting in the crowd. You agree that you won't go again because of this. You say:

The trouble is nowadays that there _____

e You are a lazy student! Your teacher thinks you could make more progress. At the end of the year, your teacher gives you your report and says:

That's a bit better. But you still _____

Countables and uncountables ▶ SB p118

5 Choose the most suitable expression from the words underlined.

a I like your hair. (It is)/They are a lovely colour.

b Chicken is/are more tasty than beef, I think.

c Here is/are the news for today, Tuesday 19th December.

d The surprise was/were so unexpected that everyone laughed.

e My money is/are in my handbag on the table.

f The information she gave him was/were not completely accurate.

6 Choose between *a/an* and *some* in each sentence.

a Could you give me an/(some) information about trips to Holland?

b They gave us a/some advice about our holiday.

c I looked at the menu and decided to eat a/some chicken.

d She is working at the moment as a/some news-reader.

e Last year he became a/some furniture salesman.

f We had a/some surprise when she suddenly turned up at the party.

Conditional 1 ▶ SB p111

7 Rewrite each sentence beginning as shown, so that the meaning remains the same.

a If the train isn't late, we'll be there at six.

We won't _be there at six if the train is late._

b I'll call the police unless you go away!

If _____

c You'll pass the exam, if you don't do anything silly.

You won't _____

d You won't start feeling better if you don't take more exercise.

If you _____

e If you don't leave now, you'll miss the bus.

You won't _____

f I'm not coming, if you don't pay for my ticket!

If you pay _____

Have, make or *take*

8 Complete each sentence with the most suitable form of *have, make* or *take*.

a Every time he __makes__ a mistake, he tries to correct himself.

b Please don't _____ fun of her, she will be embarrassed.

c We're _____ a party on Saturday. Would you like to come?

d If you _____ more exercise, you will feel better.

e I'm thinking of _____ some photos of those buildings.

f Whenever they have a party they _____ too much noise.

Text organisers

9 Put one of the words or phrases given in the list into each space in the text. Use each word or phrase once only.

although   as well as this   besides   first of all   finally   for example
however   on the other hand

What is your view of the future? Many people predict that education will change greatly over the next fifty years. [1] __First of all__, students will be able to study at home by using a computer which will teach them anything they want to know. [2] _____, the computer will keep them in touch with their teachers, and reward them when they do well. [3] _____, when a student does well in a test, the computer will show half an hour of the student's favourite rock group as a reward. [4] _____ learning at home, every student will also take part in sports in the local sports centre. [5] _____, these are not the only kinds of changes which will take place. Education will continue for as long as the student wishes to learn. [6] _____ there will be fewer jobs in the future, there will be a greater need for highly qualified experts, so everyone will be encouraged to study for as long as possible. [7] _____, the actual subjects students will study in the future will be very different, and things which only university students study today will be easy subjects for seven-year-olds. [8] _____, some features of education as we know it today will remain the same. There will still be exams, unfortunately. And there will be students who have to be punished by the computer!

Writing

10 Write 100 words about the way you imagine the future for **one** of these topics.

    living in a large city   travelling
    daily life   work

_____
_____
_____
_____
_____
_____
_____
_____
_____
_____

Skills: Reading and Listening ▶ SB p49: further activities

11 a Find these words and phrases. Check their meanings in a dictionary if necessary.

operator call receiver dial telephone directory get through

ring off

b Use six of the words in **a** once only in this text. Put the verbs in a suitable tense.

Last weekend I decided to [1] _____ a friend of mine who lives in Japan. I [2] _____ the number, and to my surprise I [3] _____ almost immediately. But it must have been a wrong number, because someone speaking German answered the phone. I tried again, and the same thing happened, so I [4] _____ immediately, and called the [5] _____ to check the number. He told me to look it up in the [6] _____ , which wasn't much help. I decided to write a letter instead.

Pronunciation and listening

12 a 🔊 Listen and repeat these questions. Try to copy the intonation of each question.

1 Excuse me, is it all right if I use the phone?
2 You know her number, don't you?
3 Are you waiting to make a call?
4 What's the area code for Cambridge?
5 Where's the telephone directory?

b 🔊 Listen to the extract from Skills: Listening and Writing SB p53, activity 1. In each space, write the word you hear.

I don't think we'll have cars any more, they _____ _____ _____ _____ _____ and make a lot of noise and pollution and all that. So I should think _____ _____ _____ _____ some kind of public system, but not buses like we've got now. Maybe some kind of electric railway, either underground or maybe _____ _____ _____ _____ . Everything will be electric, but I think the power will come from the sun, or maybe even from the wind, because there won't be _____ _____ _____ _____ _____ .

I don't think things will be _____ _____ _____ . I expect we'll all be sitting at home and watching some kind of super satellite TV. I don't think I'm _____ _____ _____ _____ really. There'll be computers everywhere and life will be all about pushing buttons.

Vocabulary consolidation

13 Make lists of words you have learned in this unit under these headings:

Science and Technology   **Uncountable Nouns**

Progress Test 2

Units 3, 4, 5 and 6

1   Put each verb into either past simple or present perfect simple.

   a A I (leave) _____ some shoes here yesterday for repair. Are they ready?
      B Sorry, I (not do) _____ them yet.

   b (you see) _____ my wallet? I'm sure I (put) _____ it here on this table.

   c Would you like some cake? I (buy) _____ it this morning. Thanks, but I (just have) _____ my lunch.

   d How long (you stay) _____ in Paris last year? And (you enjoy) _____ it?

   e I (not go) _____ to the theatre since I (see) _____ *Hamlet* in 1988.

   f I can't play football for a while because I (break) _____ my ankle.

   g It's ages since I last (write) _____ to you.

   h I (visit) _____ Hungary ten years ago.

   i I (not realise) _____ that you and Ruth are friends. How long (you know) _____ her?

   15 marks

2   Put each verb into either past simple or past continuous.

   a I (go) _____ into the kitchen to make some tea, but while the kettle (boil) _____ the phone (ring) _____ .

   b While Harry (wait) _____ for Jean outside the cinema, he (met) _____ an old friend of his and they (have) _____ a long conversation about their schooldays.

   c Last summer I (stay) _____ with some friends in Belgium. Every day I (go) _____ to look at old buildings, and (draw) _____ people in the street.

d A What (you do) _____ when the accident (happen) _____?

   B I (run) _____ to the phonebox and (call) _____ an ambulance.

e When she (ring) _____ the doorbell I (have) _____ a bath, and I couldn't answer.

15 marks

3 Rewrite each sentence beginning as shown, so that the meaning remains the same.

   a My house is not as large as yours.

   Your house _____

   b Nowhere is more expensive than this restaurant.

   This restaurant is the _____

   c This film was better than the last one.

   The last film was not _____

   d All the other players on the field were better than Jim.

   Jim was the _____

   e The second question was easier than the first one.

   The first question was _____

5 marks

4 Put *a/an*, or *the* in each space or leave the space blank.

   a I think I know _____ place where _____ robbers hid _____ painting.

   b Clive speaks _____ French with _____ Australian accent.

   c She's _____ computer programmer and she lives in _____ London.

   d When I was at _____ school I liked _____ history a lot.

   e Robin Hood used to steal _____ money from _____ rich and give it to _____ poor.

   f Catherine plays _____ piano quite well, although she doesn't have _____ teacher.

   g There was _____ serious fire in _____ prison yesterday.

   h Sheila often goes to _____ cinema, but she doesn't like _____ horror films.

9 marks

41

5 Complete each mini-dialogue.

a A Gosh, this bag is really heavy.

  B Shall _____

b A I'd like to go sailing tomorrow, but the weather might be bad.

  B If _____ home.

c A How do you see yourself in ten years time?

  B I expect _____

d A Is this your first time in London?

  B No, I _____ before.

e A Why didn't you answer the phone?

  B Sorry, I _____ my homework.

5 marks

6 Put one suitable word into each space.

a I didn't have _____ money to travel by plane so I went by train.

b I asked him for _____ advice but he said he was busy.

c They told her she was _____ young to see the film.

d We wanted to go swimming, but there were too _____ people on the beach, and the sea wasn't warm _____ .

e I failed my exams because I spent too _____ time playing football and too _____ time studying.

f As for languages, I know _____ German, but I don't know very _____ .

g They bought _____ furniture, but the house didn't have _____ beds for all the bedrooms.

7 marks

Unit 7 The time of your life

▶ Obligation
▶ Possibility
▶ Purpose clauses

Obligation and possibility ▶ SB p115, 116

1 Rewrite each sentence so that it includes the word given in brackets, and the meaning remains the same.

a I'm sure that isn't John's bike. (CAN'T)
   That can't be John's bike.

b Perhaps I'll see you again next week. (MIGHT)
   _____

c I'm sure you know what I mean. (MUST)
   _____

d It's possible that it will break, you know. (COULD)
   _____

e Perhaps I won't go to Japan this summer. (MIGHT)
   _____

f I'm sure this is the Tower of London. (MUST)
   _____

Obligation, possibility and advice ▶ SB p114, 115, 116

2 Rewrite each sentence beginning as shown, so that the meaning remains the same. Use *had better, have to,* or *must*.

a I think it would be a good idea if you went home now.
   You had _better go home now._

b I'm sure this is the place where I lost my wallet.
   This must _____

c Is it really necessary for you to go shopping again?
   Do you _____

d I think it's important for you to stop smoking!
   You _____

43

e The rules say that you go back to the first square.

You _____

f It's not necessary for him to work on Saturdays.

He _____

Purpose clauses ▶ SB p116

3 Make a sentence from each pair given, using either the infinitive of purpose:

*He wanted to see his friends. He went there.
Why did he go? – He went there <u>to see</u> his friends.*

or using *so that + could*:

*She wanted to see her friends. They went there.
Why did they go? – They went there <u>so that she could</u> see her friends.*

Begin as shown. Make any other necessary changes.

a Peter wanted to buy a new motorbike. He saved all his pocket money.

Peter saved *all his money to buy a new motorbike.*

b Jack wanted to use the phone. Sue turned down the television.

Sue turned _____

c Jim didn't want people to recognise him. He covered his face.

Jim covered _____

d Bill wanted to look up a word. He picked up the dictionary.

Bill picked up _____

e Julie wanted to have a shower. She went into the bathroom.

Julie went _____

f Martin wanted people to be able to see in the dark. He lit some candles.

Martin lit _____

It and there ▶ SB p121

4 Rewrite each sentence so that it includes the word given in brackets, and the meaning remains the same.

a I think there might be some snow tomorrow. (IT)
  I think it might snow tomorrow.

b This street has a pub on the corner. (THERE)

c This town is small but interesting. (IT)

d I see no point in waiting all afternoon. (THERE)

e The post office is not far from here. (IT)

f We have to do a lot of work. (THERE)

g Today is very warm. (IT)

h Do we have time for a drink?. (THERE)

So and such ▶ SB p117

5 Rewrite each sentence beginning as shown, so that the meaning remains the same.

a He went home to bed because he was very tired.
  He was so _tired that he went home to bed._

b It was a sunny day so we decided to go for a swim.
  It was such _____

c She ate a lot and began to feel ill.
  She ate so _____

d She ate a lot and began to feel ill.
  She ate such _____

e I haven't had a good time like that for ages.

I haven't had such _____

f The case was so heavy that I couldn't lift it.

It was such _____

Too and enough ▶ SB p117

6 Comment on each situation, using an adjective and *too* or *enough*.

a You have to be over sixteen to see this film. You are fourteen.

You're not old enough to see this film.

b I can't go swimming today. It's really cold!

_____

c I'm not very tall. I can't reach that shelf.

_____

d This piece of string is one metre long. I need two metres.

_____

e I can't drink this tea now! I'll burn my mouth.

_____

f Sorry, you can't go in. The lesson has started.

_____

Phrasal/multi-word verbs ▶ SB p121

7 Match each verb from the list with one of the explanations.

break down   give up   look up   pick (someone) up   try on
deal with   turn up   pass out   put (someone) up
get on with   look forward to pick up   run out of

a think of the future with pleasure
b provide food and somewhere to sleep
c stop working (machine)
d wear clothes to see if they fit
e stop doing a habitual activity
f lift from the floor
g do business with or take action about
h faint, lose consciousness
i have good relationship with
j arrive (perhaps unexpectedly)
k collect from house in a car
l find information in a book
m have none left

8 Complete each sentence with one of the verbs from question 7.

a When I visited London some old friends ___put___ me ___up___ for a week.

b I like the people I work with, and I _____ them very well.

c He had only driven a few miles when his new car _____ .

d You'll have to have black coffee because I _____ milk.

e Every year I always _____ my Christmas holiday.

f In her job she has to _____ customers' complaints.

g I dropped my keys and a passer-by _____ them _____ .

h We invited everyone we knew to the party but nobody _____ .

i If you like I can _____ you _____ and we can go together.

j That coat is too small, you should have _____ it _____ in the shop.

Writing

9 Write 100 words about your holiday last year. Include details about:

– how you got there
– who was with you
– where you stayed
– how you spent the time
– what you most liked or disliked

_____
_____
_____
_____
_____
_____

Skills: Reading and Listening   ▶ SB p58: further activities

10 a Find these words in the text. Check their meanings in a dictionary.

damaged   restored   attraction   reconstructed   site   excavation   preserved   formerly

b Use one of the words from question a in each sentence.

1 The main _____ of the town is the castle.

2 The medieval castle was _____ used as a prison.

3 Parts of the city wall, which were in ruins, have recently been _____ ,

4 The dining hall has been _____ to its original condition.

5 The gardens with their oak trees were _____ by storms.

6 Next to the castle, the _____ of a temple has been discovered.

7 Archaeologists are now carrying out a/an _____ of the temple.

8 They have discovered wall paintings, which have been _____ for hundreds of years.

Pronunciation and listening

11 a Listen and repeat these words.

whistle	castle	dangerous	ridiculous
weather	feather	gesture	structure
plumber	thumb	thought	bought

b Listen to the extract from Skills: Listening and Writing SB p62, activity 1. In each space, write the word you hear.

I remembered there was a, a very nice campsite just outside Paris which I visited with my family as a child. So I decided I would book that in advance because it was high season, middle of August, um and _____ _____ _____ _____ _____ because we were really very squashed into this campsite. Um the _____ _____ _____ _____ , is that you don't have the luxuries that you would have in a hotel. Um . . . the facilities were fairly good but the showers _____ _____ _____ _____ _____ even though they claimed in the brochure that they would be hot, they weren't really, um . . . and you have to wait for your shower and if you need the toilet in the night _____ _____ _____ _____ _____ _____ _____ across the campsite to the nearest wash area. Um . . . but we were right, our tent was right next to the river which was very nice except for the mosquitoes, the mosquitoes were huge.

Vocabulary consolidation

12 Make lists of words you have learned in this unit under these headings:

Holidays   **Travel**

Unit 8 Meet the family

▶ Reported statements

Vocabulary: character and feelings

1 Study the list of words for describing character and feelings. Use a dictionary if necessary. Mark the words as positive (+) or negative (−).

lonely	worried	easygoing	strict
lazy	unreliable	shy	bored

2 Complete each sentence with a word from the list in question 1.

a She can't find anything to interest her. She always feels __bored__ .

b He's so _____ that he goes red when anyone talks to him.

c Our teacher lets us do anything we want. He is very _____ .

d I don't know anyone in this town, and I feel a bit _____ .

e He's so _____ ! He spends all his time sleeping instead of studying.

f You don't know if she will do what she promises. She is very _____ .

g My boss never lets me leave early. He is very _____ .

h I've had this pain in my arm for a week now, and I feel a bit _____ .

Reported Statements   ▶ SB p113

3 Rewrite each sentence beginning as shown, so that the meaning remains the same.

a 'John, don't wait for me because I won't be back until eight.'
   Liz told John _not to wait for her because she wouldn't be back until eight._

b The teacher told the class that they had done very well in the test.
   'Well, everybody, _____'

c 'I'm leaving at six, Joe, after I've finished the painting.'
   Lucy told Joe _____

d Sally told Robert that when she saw him she would tell him the news.
   'Robert, when _____

e 'Jane, I can't talk for long because I'm cooking the dinner.'
   Michael told Jane _____

f Cathy said that her dog had been chasing her neighbour's cat.

'This dog of mine _____

g 'I was just too tired to go out, Bill.'

Sarah explained to Bill _____

h 'After I've finished school I'm going to travel round the world.'

Ann told us _____

Changes in reported speech ▶ SB p113

4 Choose the most suitable expression from the words underlined.

a She told Sam she would see him the following day.
'Sam, I'll see (you)/them/him another day/(tomorrow)/yesterday.'

b 'Put this on that shelf, will you?'
She told him to put that/it/himself on that/this/the shelf.

c 'I have to finish this now.'
He said that he had to finish this/that/it once/now/then.

d He told John that he hadn't seen her there the night before.
'I didn't see him/her/you there tonight/last night/at night.

e 'Bring these books back this afternoon, please.'
She asked him to bring these/the/those books back that/the afternoon.

f 'I wasn't here yesterday.'
She said that she hadn't been there/here yesterday/then/the day before.

5 Rewrite these sentences as reported statements, changing the reference and time words as necessary.

a 'John, put this on that desk, please,' said Kate.

   Kate asked John to put it on the desk.

b 'I'll see you here tomorrow, Sue,' said Brian.

   _____

c 'I took this to the cleaner's last week,' she said.

   _____

d 'She's joining me here next year,' said Jim.

   _____

e 'The last thing I want is to leave you here, Mary,' said Paul.

   _____

f 'I left this on that table yesterday,' said Graham.

   _____

Writing: reported speech ▶ SB p113

6 Read the news reports and then answer the questions below.

'And now, more news about the government's plans for dealing with the latest economic crisis. Reports are rather confusing at the moment, but a government spokesman had this to say to our political correspondent, James Harding.'

'The Prime Minister has been discussing his plans with other ministers and he has reached a number of important decisions. First of all, the price of cigarettes will rise by 20%, but the price of beer and other alcoholic drinks will remain the same. The old age pension will go up by 10%, but not until after Christmas. Ministers have agreed to stop all pay rises for government employees. They have also decided to meet in a week's time to make a final decision about income tax. The Prime Minister feels that there is no need to increase income tax by more than 2% or 3%.'

'Since we recorded that interview, James Harding has also spoken to the Prime Minister, who gave a rather different view.'

'I would first of all like everyone to know that the government has not made any decisions yet about the economy. I have not spoken to any ministers yet, but as soon as I do, and as soon as we reach a decision, we will make an announcement. I can tell you, however, some of the things that will not happen. For example, there will be no increase in the price of cigarettes, as the last increase was only two months ago, and it would be unfair to raise the price again so soon. Also, there will definitely not be a rise in income tax. As far as pensions go, I feel that the old age pensioners deserve more, and I think they will get a rise of at least 15% before Christmas. There has been no discussion about pay rises for government employees. I am meeting other ministers tomorrow, and we will make our final decisions then.'

What differences are there between what the spokesman said, and what the Prime Minister said about these topics:

meetings with ministers   decisions about prices   income tax
decisions about pay rises   old age pensions

_____
_____
_____
_____
_____
_____
_____
_____

Skills: Reading and Listening ▶ SB p67: further activities

7 a Find these words or phrases in the text. Check their meanings in a dictionary if necessary.

handle (a problem)   manners   it gets (me) down   confess   get on with   lose your temper   look up to someone   have nothing in common (with someone)

b Rewrite each sentence, using one of the words or phrases from **a**.

1 My boss annoyed me so much that I suddenly became very angry.
   My boss annoyed me so much that I lost my temper.

2 Jack is a very helpful boy, and his behaviour is excellent.
   _____

3 Mandy and Paul have decided not to get married because they are not interested in the same things.
   _____

4 When nobody writes to me it makes me feel really miserable.
   _____

5 Brenda is very good at dealing with emergencies.
   _____

6 Martin admitted to Sue that he had been telling lies about her.
   _____

7 Katherine and Diane have always admired their father.
   _____

8 Derek doesn't have a very good relationship with his sister.
   _____

52

Pronunciation and listening

8 **a** 🔲 Listen and repeat these words. Ⓒircle the syllable with the main stress in each word.

conclusion   reasonable   wonderful   pillion
unfortunate   deduction   noticeable   relation

b 🔲 Listen to the extract from Skills: Reading and Listening SB p68, activity 7. In each space, write the word you hear.

I found that hard to believe, and later I talked to the boys' mother. I told her what her husband _____ _____ , and she burst out laughing. When I asked her why, she told me that her sons had done _____ _____ _____ _____ that their father knew nothing about. I asked her for some examples, and it turned out that the boys had done _____ _____ _____ _____ smoking and drinking in secret, both at home, and when out with their friends. But she said that she hadn't been angry with them when she found out. She hadn't forgotten _____ _____ _____ _____ to be a teenager, and remembered getting into trouble herself, and being locked in her room. She said she had decided when she had children that she wouldn't _____ _____ _____ _____ her parents had made.

Vocabulary consolidation

9 Make lists of words you have learned in this unit under these headings:

Personal Qualities   **Family Relationships**

53

Unit 9 All in the mind

▶ Conditional 1
▶ Conditional 2

Conditional 1 ▶ SB p111

1 Complete the comment on each situation.

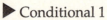

a We are in a small boat, the kind that sinks easily. I want to stand up. You say:

'If _you stand up, the boat will sink._'

b We are in England. We are going for a picnic tomorrow. It often rains. We plan not to go in that case. You say:

'If it _____

c You are carrying a glass vase, the kind that breaks easily. You are not being very careful. I say:

'If you _____

d Your boss gets angry when you talk to friends on the phone, but he doesn't always catch you. You are on the phone to a friend now. You say:

'If my _____

e You are in the post office. You want to send a present to France for a friend's birthday. The clerk tells you to send it express to make sure that it arrives in time. She says:

'If you don't _____

f You like sweets very much, and are putting on too much weight. Your doctor tells you to lose weight by giving up sweets, and says:

'If you _____

g It is winter in Scotland, and you don't have any warm clothes. A friend lends you a thick coat to make you feel warmer, and says:

'You won't _____

h A friend wants to borrow some money and promises to pay you back next week. She says:

'If you _____

Conditional 1 and 2 ▶ SB p111

2 For each sentence **a** to **j** choose the most suitable ending **1** to **10**.

a If I lived in a house as big as yours . . .   _4_

b If I have time when I go shopping on Saturday morning . . .   _____

c If I was alone in the house and the electricity went off . . .   _____

d If I have a birthday party this year . . .   _____

e If I change my mind about going to the theatre . . .   _____

f If I had more free time during the week . . .   _____

g If I can find some fresh fish at the market tomorrow . . .   _____

h If I were taller and a lot fitter . . .   _____

1 . . . I'd light some candles and wait for it to go on again.
2 . . . I'll give you a ring early on Tuesday evening.
3 . . . I'll cook a nice dinner.
4 . . . I'd buy more furniture and some carpets.
5 . . . I'll invite all the people from my English class.
6 . . . I'd agree to play in the basketball team.
7 . . . I'd go more often to the cinema and the theatre.
8 . . . I'll buy those batteries you need for your cassette player.

Vocabulary: character

3 Match each of the words given with the sentence which best explains it. Use a dictionary if necessary.

aggressive   confident   mean   selfish   rude
brave   honest   reliable shy   generous

a If you are like this, then people will trust you.   _honest_

b You find it difficult to talk to others.   _____

c You are happy when you give things to others.   _____

d You attack people with words, or fists!   _____

e You think only of one person – yourself!   _____

f If you were more polite, it would help.   _____

g You would know what to do in a dangerous situation.   _____

h You believe in your own ability.   _____

i If you make a promise, you keep it.   _____

j You don't like spending money, I'm afraid.   _____

Giving advice ▶ SB p114

4 Complete the mini-dialogues by adding some advice.

a **A** I don't know whether to buy the red one or the green one.
   B If I _were you, I'd buy the green one._

b **A** There are two trains, one at 2.00 and one at 4.30.
   B I think you _____

c **A** I've got a terrible headache.
   B Why _____

d **A** I'm going to paint my living-room purple.
   B _____ , if I were you.

e **A** It's really hot, isn't it. Shall we go jogging?
   B I don't _____

f **A** I feel exhausted. I've been working too hard.
   B I'd take a holiday _____

g **A** I really don't know what to do. There is water all over the floor in the kitchen, and I think a pipe has burst.
   B I think you _____

h **A** This food is terrible. And the waiter is really rude.
   B Why _____

Conditional 1 and 2 ▶ SB p111

5 Rewrite each sentence beginning as shown, so that the meaning remains the same.

a I haven't got a stamp. I can't post my letter.
  I could _post my letter if I had a stamp._

b Don't worry about falling in. There's a life-guard to rescue you.
  If _____

c I can't tell you the answer because I don't know it.
  If _____

d I'm not a farmer. It must be a lonely job.
  If I _____

e We're leaving tomorrow – but not if there's a change in the weather.
  We won't _____

Writing

6 Study the paragraph below, and then write similar paragraphs about the topics given. Use the ideas given.

I've always wanted to own a dog, but my parents say this is impossible. I still dream about it a lot. If I had a dog, I would take it for a walk every morning before I went to school. I would buy its food, and feed it twice a day. I would also teach my dog to do tricks. I would play with it, and at the weekend I would take it to the park. I would also brush it and occasionally give it a bath.

I've always wanted to own a motorbike _____
_____
_____
_____
_____
_____

7 Write other paragraphs about a flat or house of your own, **or** a musical instrument.

_____
_____
_____
_____
_____
_____

Skills: Reading and Listening ▶ SB p76: further activities

8 a Find these words in the text. Check their meanings in a dictionary if necessary.

direct   nervous   lively   sympathetic   caring   self-conscious   embarrassed   realistic

b Match each word in **a** with one of these explanations.

Someone who . . .

1 understands the feelings of others is _sympathetic_

2 always thinks about how others see them is _____

3 says exactly what they feel is _____

4 feels worried all the time is _____

5 has a lot of energy is _____.

6 takes time to help other people is _____.

7 sees things the way they are is _____.

8 always feels uncomfortable or ashamed is _____.

Pronunciation and listening

9 a 🔊 Listen to these words and (circle) the sound schwa /ə/.

important vital communication nervous posture observe sufferer negative

b 🔊 Listen again and <u>underline</u> the main stress in each word.

c 🔊 Listen to the extract from Skills: Reading and Listening SB p77, activity 7. In each space write the word you hear.

Interviewer: David, you were _____ _____ _____ _____ when you were young, weren't you.

David: Yes I'm afraid I was _____ _____ _____ _____ who was always fighting and causing trouble at school. It was just the way I grew up, and I didn't really see it as a problem. I was always very noisy, both _____ _____ _____ _____ school. My mother didn't let me in the house a lot of the time, and of course I was always _____ _____ _____ _____ school with the teachers. I guess I was just very aggressive, you know, always looking for trouble. I remember _____ _____ _____ _____ telling me that every time I opened my mouth I _____ _____ _____ _____ _____ .

Vocabulary consolidation

10 Make lists of words you have learned in this unit under these headings:

Positive Personal Qualities   **Negative Personal Qualities**

Unit 10 Just good friends

▶ Relative clauses
▶ Reported speech

Vocabulary: personal characteristics

1 Complete each sentence by using a word from the list. Use each word only once. Use a dictionary if necessary.

determined lively tolerant worried bored frank suspicious cheerful jealous patient

a Susan still hasn't got over her cold and I'm a bit ___worried___ .

b Tell me exactly what you think of me. I want you to be _____ .

c There's nothing to do in this place. I feel really _____ .

d My parents were very _____ , and let me do things they didn't agree with.

e Don't look so unhappy! Try to be a bit more _____ .

f The policeman saw a strange man waiting by the bank and became _____ .

g She managed to pass her exams in the end because she was so _____ .

h He is full of energy, and new ideas. He's a very _____ person.

i When she saw her boyfriend kissing another girl she felt very _____ .

j You have to do this job slowly and carefully and be very _____ .

Vocabulary: word building

2 Use a dictionary to complete this table.

Adjective	Noun	Adjective	Noun
determined	_____	frank	_____
jealous	_____	patient	_____
suspicious	_____	bored	_____
tolerant	_____	worried	_____

3 Complete these sentences with words you found in question 2. Use a dictionary if necessary. The word may be in a plural form.

a A carefree person is someone who has no ___worries___ .

b I have a _____ that Paul is not telling the truth.

c Anyone who suffers from _____ should take up a hobby.

d I would expect complete _____ from someone who was a close friend.

e I tend to lose _____ with people who ask me to repeat instructions.

f People who succeed in this job have to show a lot of _____ .

g Society should show _____ towards young people who break the law.

h The man who loved her suffered from terrible _____ .

Who, what and how

4 Put *who, what* or *how* into each space.

When I woke up, I couldn't remember [1] _____ had happened. [2] _____ had I got there, and [3] _____ had brought me? And [4] _____ was the matter with my poor head? I didn't know [5] _____ had hit me, but they had certainly found a sensitive spot. I badly needed two aspirins and a pot of black coffee, but I didn't know [6] _____ I was going to find them. Anyone [7] _____ has been in this situation will know the feeling. I didn't have any idea [8] _____ I was going to escape, but when I did I knew [9] _____ I was going to visit. The mysterious Natasha Tildesley. And I knew [10] _____ I was going to ask her.

Relative clauses ▶ SB p116

5 Circle each *who* which can be left out in these sentences. (In more formal or written English *whom* would be used in these cases).

a This is a photo of someone (who) I met while I was on holiday.
b Are you the person who called me late last night?
c I'd like to talk to someone who has visited China.

d Nobody knows who left this parcel here this morning.
e John is the only person in this office who I can trust.
f When I find out who did this, there will be trouble.
g She is the person who owns that black dog.
h The police officer who I spoke to before isn't on duty today.

Advice, making suggestions, making introductions ▶ SB p114

6 Complete these mini-dialogues by following the instructions.

a **A** (invite your friend to your party on Saturday)

I'm having a party on Saturday, would you like to come?

B That's very kind of you, but I'm already going out.

b **A** (offer your friend a cup of tea)

_____

B No thanks, I've just had one.

c **A** I feel really awful. I can't stop coughing.

B (advise your friend to give up smoking)

_____

d **A** What could we do tonight? I feel like going out somewhere.

B (suggest going to the cinema)

_____

e **A** (introduce yourself to a stranger)

_____

B Oh hello. I'm Jackie. And this is Barry.

Reported questions ▶ SB p113

7 Rewrite each sentence beginning as shown, so that the meaning remains the same.

a 'Where are you going, Sue?' Joe asked.

Joe asked Sue _where she was going._

b 'Have you seen the new film on at the Odeon?' Peter asked them.

Peter asked them _____

c 'Why didn't you tell me before, Nick?' said Frances.

Frances asked Nick _____

d 'Did I leave my gloves here last night?' Paula asked him.

Paula asked him _____

e 'Are you going home when the lesson finishes?' Keith asked Jill.

Keith asked Jill _____

f 'Who usually sits next to you in English?' Sheila's mother asked.

Sheila's mother asked her _____

g 'Are you going to be here next year?' Michael asked Judith.

Michael asked Judith _____

h 'Why are you crying, Charlie?' his sister asked him.

Charlie's sister asked him _____

Vocabulary

8 Complete each sentence with a suitable verb.

a I can't do this on my own. Could you ____give____ me a hand?

b At Christmas I always eat too much and _____ on weight.

c Stop playing with that electronic game! It's _____ me crazy.

d The car could not stop on the wet road and _____ into a tree.

e She was very happy when she heard she had _____ the examination.

f If you _____ your mind about coming for the weekend, let me know.

g Could you _____ me some advice? I don't know what to do.

h Quite honestly, I think there _____ no point in continuing.

Describing people

9 Put one suitable word in each space.

This is a description of my [1] ____best____ friend, Keith. We have known each [2] _____ for a long time, ever [3] _____ we went to school together. Keith is tall, [4] _____ fair hair and blue eyes. He usually wears casual [5] _____ . He is usually cheerful, and is rather talkative. [6] _____ I like about him, is that he is a [7] _____ listener, and is very frank too. We [8] _____ like films and dancing, and sometimes we [9] _____ the evening with other friends. Keith works as a police officer. He [10] _____ happy, but sometimes he worries about his job.

Writing

10 Study these illustrations. Imagine that you know these people. Write a paragraph about each one, like the paragraph in question 9. Include information about:

a physical appearance
b character
c life, job, likes and dislikes
d other ideas

a This is a description of _____

_____
_____
_____
_____
_____
_____
_____

b This is a description of _____

_____
_____
_____
_____
_____
_____
_____

Skills: Reading and Listening ▶ SB p85, activity 2: further activities

11 a Find these words in the text. Check their meanings in a dictionary if necessary.

take place   single   insist on   cruel   on and off   give up   join   date

b Use one of the words or phrases from **a** in each sentence. Put verbs in a suitable tense and form.

1 I've been building this model plane __on and off__ for the last year.

2 I tried to refuse, but the hotel porter _____ carrying my suitcase.

3 I think it's more interesting being _____ than being married!

4 Jack decided to _____ the army when he left school.

5 The robbery _____ at some time on Saturday evening.

6 They were fined £100 for treating their dog in a _____ way.

7 On their first _____ , they went to see a horror film.

8 I've decided to _____ smoking at the end of the week.

Pronunciation and listening

12 a 🎧 Listen and repeat these words.

rich   church   catch   lunch   match   huge   giant   gin   agency   reject

b 🎧 Listen to the extract from Skills: Listening and Writing SB p89, activity 5. In each space write the word you hear.

I've got a neighbour who I suppose is one of my best friends, and I think I admire her most because she says _____ _____ _____ _____ . I'm sure she would never lie to me. Even little things, like if I say ' _____ _____ _____ _____ _____ ?' she'll tell me exactly what she thinks. I think that friends have _____ _____ _____ _____ _____ , don't you? She's also the kind of person I can always depend on if I need anything – you know, _____ _____ _____ _____ _____ _____ _____ , or I can borrow some sugar, and I know she won't complain about it. _____ _____ _____ _____ _____ _____ _____ .

Vocabulary consolidation

13 Make lists of words you have learned in this unit under this heading:

Love and Marriage

Progress Test 3

Units 7, 8, 9 and 10

1 Rewrite each sentence as reported speech beginning as given.

a 'Do you want tea or coffee, John?'

Carol asked _____

b 'Don't leave your bags near the door, girls,' said the teacher.

The teacher told _____

c 'I'll help you if I have time, Mary,' said Alice.

Alice told _____

d 'I've left the money on top of the fridge, Sue,' said Alan.

Alan said _____

e 'I'm taking the 4.30 train, Harry,' said Sheila.

Sheila told _____

f 'When does the film start, Dave?' asked Patsy.

Patsy asked _____

g 'Were you here on Wednesday, Valerie?' asked Brian.

Brian asked _____

h 'Can I borrow your radio, Jack?' said Paul.

Paul asked Jack _____

i 'Has your dog had any puppies?' asked Nigel.

Nigel asked me _____

j 'I've forgotten my homework,' said Helen.

Helen told the teacher _____

10 marks

2 Rewrite each sentence using the word given, so that the meaning of the sentence remains the same.

a I'm sure that it is not Tuesday today. (CAN'T)

_____

b School uniform is not compulsory in this school. (HAVE)

_____

c I think you should stay in bed for a couple of days. (HAD)

_____

d Perhaps we'll miss the bus. (MIGHT)

_____

e I'm sure that's John over there. (MUST)

_____

10 marks

3 Complete each sentence by putting **one** word in each space.

a It was a good film but I was _____ tired _____ enjoy it.

b The car was _____ large _____ to carry all the family.

c The suitcase was _____ heavy that I _____ not lift it.

d The doctor arrived _____ late _____ help the old man.

e It was _____ an expensive restaurant that I didn't have _____ money.

f I went out _____ buy some milk but I was _____ late, the shops were closed.

g She was driving _____ fast _____ stop.

h There was not _____ time _____ finish the test.

i It snowed yesterday, and it was _____ cold _____ go out.

j I took the children to the park _____ that they _____ play football.

10 marks

4 Put each verb in brackets into a suitable tense.

a If I (have) _____ the money, I (buy) _____ a motorbike. But there is no chance, I'm afraid!

b As soon as I (hear) _____ any news, I (let) _____ you know.

c If they (keep) _____ playing as badly as this, they (lose) _____ the match!

d If I (be) _____ you, I (not spend) _____ so much time at home.

e I (give) _____ you a ring when I (get) _____ home tonight.

f Look out! If you (stand) _____ near the edge you (fall) _____ .

67

g Why don't you give up smoking? You (not feel) _____ so ill if you (not smoke) _____ .

h Don't worry. I (wait) _____ here for you until you (come) _____ back.

i If you (not stop) _____ making such a terrible noise, I (call) _____ the police.

j If more people (use) _____ bicycles, there (not be) _____ so much pollution.

10 marks

5 Put one suitable word in each space.

While I'm sitting in my office and waiting for five o'clock to arrive, I often wonder [1] _____ people will work so much in the future. I don't think that this is very likely, because [2] _____ won't be [3] _____ work for everyone, so people will probably retire when they [4] _____ fifty, or perhaps younger. And what about all the retired people? Well, they won't [5] _____ all their time sitting at home watching television. They will look [6] _____ to their retirement, because they will be able to do [7] _____ the things they always wanted to do. This has already started to happen [8] _____ some countries. Retired people take up interesting hobbies, or travel. They are much healthier [9] _____ they used to be, and they live longer. The only probably is that soon there will be [10] _____ many people who have retired that the young people will begin to feel outnumbered!

10 marks

Unit 11 What's on?

▶ Passive voice
▶ Phrasal/multi-word verbs

Passive voice ▶ SB p112

1   Change each sentence into the passive. Decide whether to include the agent (the person who did the action).

   a We make these biscuits in our Bristol factory.
      These biscuits are made in our Bristol factory.

   b Someone took all the money from the cashier's desk.

   c The company has decided to close the office on Thursday.

   d Mr Johnson will give a speech at the meeting.

   e Someone is meeting Janet at the airport.

   f We know nothing about the missing jewellery.

   g You usually sign a cheque with a pen, not with a pencil.

   h They recorded her singing live at a night-club.

2   Change these passive sentences into the active voice.

   a My cherry tree has been cut down!
      Someone has cut down my cherry tree.

   b These pullovers are made in Scotland.

   c They were rescued by a man in a fishing boat.

d She was not helped at the police station.

e This trip will be remembered by all of us.

f Their house is being sold.

g This play was written by Harold Pinter.

h Her advice was not taken by her brother.

3 Rewrite each sentence beginning as shown, so that the meaning remains the same.

a We have to organise our Christmas party.

Our Christmas party _has to be organised._

b We should invite the guests this week.

The guests _____

c We will have to telephone some of them.

Some of them _____

d We have to buy all the food.

All the food _____

e We have to put up the decorations.

The decorations _____

f We have to wrap the presents.

The presents _____

g We have to find a baby-sitter.

A baby-sitter _____

h We have to cook the turkey for a long time.

The turkey _____

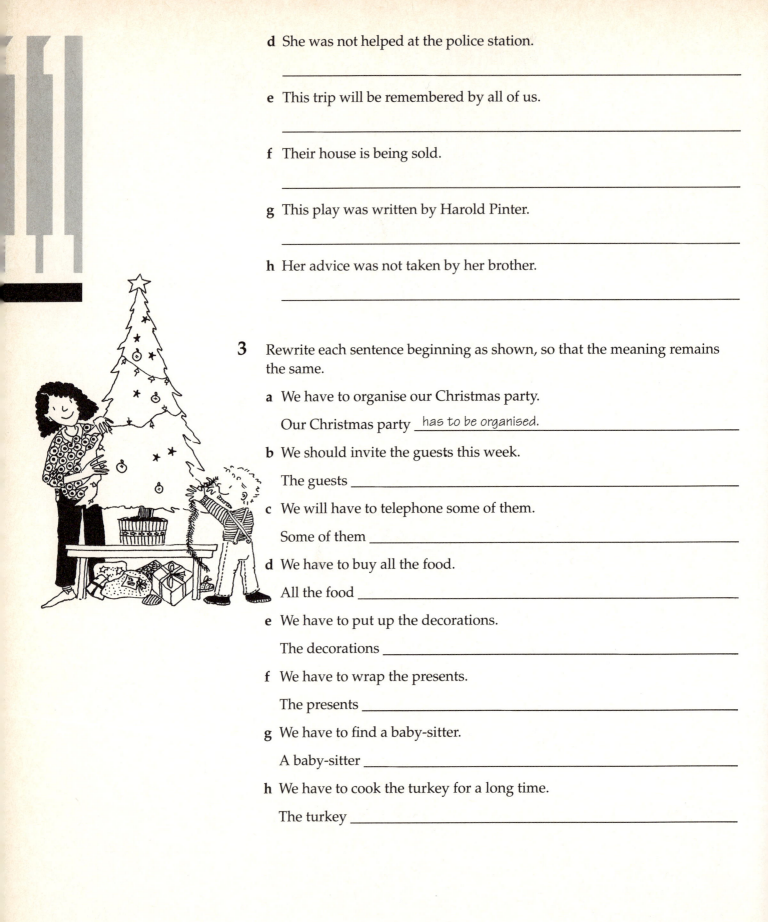

Making comparisons ▶ SB p117

4 Put a word from the list into each space, in a comparative form. Some words can be used more than once.

convenient   easy   exciting   expensive   good   interesting   relaxing   sociable

I'm not sure whether watching films is __better__ than reading books, or not. Books are certainly _____ _____ than films and probably _____ _____ too (because you keep them). On the other hand, some films are _____ _____ because of the special effects, although some people say that books can be just as _____. Going to see a film is a _____ _____ activity than sitting alone and reading, it's true. But if you don't like a book, it's much _____ to stop reading it than it is to leave the cinema! Some books are _____ than others, just as some films are. Personally, I find a good film _____ _____ than reading if I'm tired, but in general I think books are _____ _____ .

Verbs and prepositions

5 Put a preposition into each space.

a I'm going to apply __for__ this teaching job advertised in the paper.
b I'm really looking forward _____ having a good rest this summer.
c The manager sent _____ her and offered her a promotion.
d The way he keeps _____ pretending to be ill is very annoying.
e I still feel awful. I just can't get rid _____ this cold.
f He denied that he had taken part _____ the robbery.
g He saved a lot of money and has been living _____ it ever since.
h Kenneth does not join _____ class activities very much, I'm afraid.

Phrasal/multi-word verbs ▶ SB p121

6 Rewrite each sentence using a verb from the list in a suitable tense. Use each verb once only.

break down   get on with   look up   pick up   put up   run out of   try on   turn up

a I decided to find the word in the dictionary.

I decided to look up the word in the dictionary.

b I asked if I could put on the trousers to see if they fitted.

c I couldn't make the cake because we did not have any flour.

d I am good friends with my mother-in-law.

e If you like, you could sleep at our house.

f Halfway up the hill the bus stopped because something was wrong with the engine.

g You'll never guess who arrived unexpectedly at the party last night!

h Could you collect me from my house at about 9.30?

Writing

7 Study these notes which describe the advantages and disadvantages of radio and television. Use the notes to complete the paragraphs below.

Television – more entertaining, wider variety of programmes?
– more educational (for example, documentaries)?
– more exciting (for example, live programmes, films)?
but: – wastes more time? talk to others less?
Radio – easier to do other things at same time? portable?
– more relaxing?
– news more interesting?
but: – too much music?

In some ways radio is better than television because _____

_____

_____

_____

_____

On the other hand, television has some advantages _____

_____

_____

_____

_____

Skills: Reading and Listening ▶ SB p94, activity 2

8 a Find these words in the text. Check their meanings in a dictionary if necessary.

clearly   equally   eagerly   vaguely   quickly   finally

b Use each word from **a** in one of the sentences below.

1 There wasn't much traffic and we got home very _____ .

2 They shared the pizza _____ between them.

3 I have _____ realised what this word means.

4 They were _____ looking forward to the end-of-term party.

5 She is _____ the best person for this job.

6 I only _____ understood the directions she gave me.

73

c Find these words from the text, and complete the table. Use a dictionary if necessary.

Noun	Adjective	Noun	Verb
perfection	———	narration	———
———	exhausting	destruction	———
privacy	———	contribution	———

Pronunciation and listening

9 a 🔊 Listen and repeat each question. Try to copy the intonation of each question.

1 Did you like the film?
2 Who wrote this book?
3 What did you think of the play?
4 What kind of films do you like?
5 What's on at the cinema tonight?

b 🔊 Listen to the extract from Skills: Reading and Listening, activity 8. In each space, write the words you hear.

Jenny: I talked to some cinema-goers waiting outside a cinema in London. _____ _____ _____ _____ about Freddy?

Girl: A bit stupid I think, OK for young kids, but _____ _____ _____ _____ _____ that kind of film myself. I might watch one if I was really bored I suppose.

Boy: I like the violence, I mean it's done well in the films, and the make-up and the effects _____ _____ _____ . And actually they're very funny films. _____ _____ _____ _____ .

Woman: Oh no, I wouldn't let my children watch films like that, gives them nightmares for a start, and they don't really understand _____ _____ _____ _____ . I don't expect they even know that it's an actor who plays Freddy.

Vocabulary consolidation

10 Make lists of words you have learned in this unit under these headings:

Television   **Entertainment**

Unit 12 Somewhere to live

▶ Passive voice

Preferences ▶ SB p115

1 Rewrite each sentence so that it includes the word given in brackets, and the meaning remains the same.

    a For me, going to bed is better than staying up late. (RATHER)
       I'd rather go to bed than stay up late.

    b I think it's better to live in the town centre. (PREFER)

    c For me, living in a flat is better than living in a house. (RATHER)

    d He doesn't like tea, he prefers to drink coffee. (RATHER)

    e We like the idea of going by train. (RATHER)

    f It's better for me to travel by bus. (PREFER)

    g Would you rather sleep in this room? (LIKE)

    h I would prefer to leave now. (RATHER)

Passive voice ▶ SB p112

2 Rewrite each sentence so that it contains a passive verb.

    a The council says that it is going to improve our town.
       The council says that our town is going to be improved.

    b Last year they built a new library in the city centre.

    c And recently they have planted a lot of trees.

d And they are improving the swimming pool.

___

e Last year some hooligans did a lot of damage.

___

f They painted slogans on the walls outside.

___

g And they broke all the windows.

___

h Now they're going to repair all the damage.

___

Passive voice: tense contrasts ▶ SB p112

3 Put each verb in brackets into the passive voice in a suitable tense.

Now that we have settled in to our new house, I thought I'd tell you all about it. Before we bought it, it [1 own] __was owned__ by a foreigner, and [2 not live in] _____ for a long time. So we have been very busy redecorating! Since we moved in, all the rooms [3 paint] _____ , and the garden [4 reorganise] _____ . But we have had a few problems. Last week the electricity [5 cut off] _____ , and nothing could [6 do] _____ until the bill [7 pay] _____ . Next month some workmen are coming to do some building work. One wall in the living room [8 knock down] _____ , and the room [9 make] _____ larger. Then perhaps we'll have some peace and quiet. We [10 visit] _____ by some of the neighbours, but we [11 not invite back] _____ by any of them yet. I suppose they wanted to see what [12 do] _____ to the house.

Passive voice: *should* and *could be done*

4 Rewrite each sentence beginning as shown, so that the meaning remains the same.

   a They should build more blocks of flats in this city.

   More _blocks of flats should be built in this city._

   b I think they could widen this road.

   I think this _____

   c They should ban traffic from the city centre.

   Traffic _____

   d They could do something about the noise!

   Something _____

   e They should plant more trees and bushes here.

   More _____

   f They could knock down all those ugly buildings.

   All those _____

   g They should restore the old buildings.

   The old buildings _____

   h They could change the plans for the new motorway.

   The plans _____

Dialogue completion

5 Complete each mini-dialogue, according to the instructions.

   a A What do you think about that old building in the town centre?

      B (Say what you think should be done)

      I think it should be knocked down.

   b A Which would you prefer, a small house, or a large flat?

      B (Give your preference, with a reason)

      _____

   c A What was this town like a few years ago?

      B (Mention what there used to be)

      _____

77

d A Have the workmen finished everything in the house?

B (Mention something that hasn't been done)

_____

e A How do you think this town could be improved?

B (Mention something that could be done)

_____

Reading

6 You are studying English in England, and you are looking for somewhere to live. You want to share a flat or house with two friends from your language school, which is in the town centre. Study the information about four possible places to live, and answer the questions.

a Detatched house, Green Lane, 6 kms from city centre. Three large bedrooms, fully furnished, TV, video, telephone, washing machine, central heating. 20 mins from bus-stop. £150 per week.

b Small terraced house near railway station. Large living room, three small bedrooms, bathroom, kitchen, back garden. Partly furnished. Close to shops and bus-stop. 20 mins from City centre. £75 per week.

c Flat near city centre, one double and one small bedroom, on main road. Suitable for students. Kitchen, outside bathroom. Needs some repairs. £45 per week.

d Three more students wanted to share house. Own rooms, share kitchen, bathroom. Quiet house near park, 30 mins from centre. Washing machine, TV. £100 per week, including all bills.

Which is nearest to the school **a**, **b**, **c** or **d**? _____

Which houses might be noisy? _____

Which house offers the best facilities? _____

What kinds of problems could each house have?

_____
_____
_____
_____
_____

Writing

7 Continue question 6 by completing these paragraphs, explaining your reasons.

I would choose _____

_____

_____

_____

I would definitely not choose _____

_____

_____

_____

Skills: Reading and Listening ▶ SB p103: further activities

8 a Find these words in the text and complete the table.

Verb	Noun	Adjective
construct	construction	constructed
_____	restoration	_____
_____	modernisation	_____
_____	_____	carpeted
_____	_____	converted

b Find these words in the text. Check their meanings in a dictionary.

bargain   view   space   shower   central heating
mobile home   ceiling

c Use each word from **b** in one of the sentences below.

1 We don't have a coal fire, we have _____ .

2 They've been living on the beach in their _____ .

3 Water came through our _____ from the flat above.

4 There is a wonderful _____ from our bedroom window.

5 We bought a larger house because we needed more _____ .

6 I'd rather have a _____ than take a bath. It's more refreshing.

7 I only paid £80,000 for the house. It was a real _____ .

Pronunciation and listening

9 a ▭ Listen and repeat these words.

character example kitchen separate double original dealer
ceiling police licence

b ▭ Listen to the extract from Skills: Reading and Listening SB p103, activity 2. In each space, write the word you hear.

Our house as you can see is completely underground, not because _____ _____ _____ _____ _____ , but when we bought this land and decided to build a house, the local council wouldn't let us put up a proper one because it would spoil the view. Yes, I found it _____ _____ _____ _____ . Anyway, we decided that we wouldn't be beaten by them, and so we had plans made for this house. You can't see _____ _____ _____ _____ _____ _____ . Down under here the house is actually quite large. It's very warm of course, and we get some light from the roof windows, but mainly we have electric lights. It's got three bedrooms, a kitchen and a living room. I must admit _it did_ _take me a while_ _____ _____ to get used to it, but now I think it's a really nice house. We go upstairs to the garden in our house . . .

Vocabulary consolidation

10 Make lists of words you have learned in this unit under these headings:

Houses and Rooms   Contents of Rooms

Final Test

1 Put each word in brackets into a suitable tense and form.

a If you (offer) _____ him the job, he'd accept it.

b I (stay) _____ with some friends at the moment.

c As soon as she (arrive) _____ , I'll let you know.

d (you see) _____ my blue scarf anywhere?

e What (you do) _____ after the lights went out?

f If I (be) _____ you, I (try) _____ harder.

g How long (you study) _____ English?

h I (never see) _____ her before in my life!

i If you (do) _____ that again, I'll scream!

j She asked me where I (go) _____ the next day.

k At the moment of the explosion I (have) _____ my dinner.

l My purse (just steal) _____ .

m 'What (you do) _____ ?' 'I'm a nurse.

n What time (you arrive) _____ here last night?

o Do you know who she (be) _____ ?

15 marks

2 Follow the instructions for each sentence, beginning as shown.

a Give a friend some advice not to buy a new car.

I don't think _____

b Apologise for being late, and explain why.

I'm sorry _____

c Ask permission to go home early.

Could _____

d Decide to buy a pair of black shoes in a shop.

I think _____

e Suggest a visit to the zoo tomorrow.

Why _____

f Offer to carry a heavy bag for someone.

That looks heavy _____

g Promise someone to give them back the money you have borrowed.

Don't worry _____

h Ask someone politely to pass you the salt.

Do you _____

i Describe your arrangements for tomorrow.

I'm _____

j Suggest a solution to the traffic problem in your town.

I think that _____

10 marks

3   Put each verb in brackets into a suitable tense and form.

Last year I [1 have] _____ a piece of good luck. One day I [2 work] _____ in the bank as usual, when I [3 get] _____ a phone call from the football pools company. They [4 tell] _____ me I [5 win] _____ a large amount of money on the football pools. A few weeks later I [6 decide] _____ to give up work and buy a house in the country. Now I [7 live] _____ in a small village in the west of England. Since I [8 move] _____ to the country I [9 learn] _____ a lot about wild animals and flowers. I [10 not have] _____ time for that kind of thing when I [11 live] _____ in London. I [12 also change] _____ my daily routine a great deal. Now I [13 spend] _____ most of my day painting. In the last few months I [14 paint] _____ some quite good portraits of my neighbours, and next month I [15 have] _____ an exhibition in a nearby town. Sometimes I [16 miss] _____ my old life, but I [17 not go] _____ back to London for months. I [18 think] _____ that most people [19 do] _____ the same as me if they [20 have] _____ the chance.

20 marks

4   Rewrite each sentence beginning as shown, so that the meaning remains the same.

a John can drive really well.

John is a _____

b Sue isn't as tall as Karen.

Karen is much _____

82

c I've got long hair.

My hair _____

d You're too young to watch this film.

You're not _____

e I think you should take your raincoat with you.

I think you had _____

f It's not necessary for you to be here early.

You don't _____

g I'm sure this isn't the right station.

This can't _____

h Someone has to clean the windows.

The windows _____

i I started reading this book two hours ago.

I've _____

j 'What have you done with my keys, Elaine?' asked Steve.

Steve asked Elaine _____

10 marks

5 Put one suitable word in each space.

a Jack waited _____ Sheila outside the cinema _____ ages.

b Two years _____ I got this job and I've worked here ever _____ .

c My house is _____ the pub and the shop _____ the end of the street.

d When Dave arrived _____ work he found a visitor _____ his office.

e She's been feeling ill a lot _____ , but she won't send _____ the doctor.

f Look it _____ in the dictionary. There's one _____ that shelf.

g Larry has lived _____ his own _____ he got divorced.

h _____ you get home you should go straight _____ bed.

i You should get rid _____ this ticket, it's out _____ date.

j I'm really looking _____ to staying _____ home tomorrow evening.

10 marks

83

Student's Book Word List

abroad 79
absolutely 102
accommodation 62
according to 105
actually 7
admire 1
advertisement 34
advise 79
affect 52
afford 21
aggressive 78
alarm clock 61
allow 15
aloud 3
ambulance 61
annoy 72
apologise 87
apply for 38
architect 100
arrange 15
authorities 97

bad-tempered 78
balance 92
ban (v) 102
bark (v) 74
bearded 88
believe in 52
be to blame 82
blanket 57
block of flats 102
bored 57
break-down 44
bring up 97
bucket 106
burglar 24
bus stop 25

cabbage 28
calculator 7
camera 11
cancel 99
cause trouble 88
chain 34
channel 46
cheerful 89
check 92
chop (n) 28
coach (n) 60
coincidence 25
colleague 83
collect 60
come round 97

comfortable 60
complain 102
compose 96
confidence 52
construct 42
convenient 34
cooker 106
couple 66
crash into 44
crazy 7
criminal 54
crossing 45
crowded 57
cushion 106
cut down (e.g. a tree) 102
cut off (e.g. power) 105

daily 2
out of date 69
deal with 11
in debt 79
department 17
description 25
detect 97
develop 97
direct (v) 96
directions 20
disadvantage 17
disappear 20
divorce (v) 66
do without 97
drawer 106
drive crazy 7
drunk 66
duty 11

easy-going 69
economical 34
editor 17
election 51
emergency 11
employer 15
entertainment 96
environment 48
estate (housing estate) 102
everyday (adj) 3
exactly 7
expect 69
experience (n) 38

facing 102
fare 21
favourite (adj) 1
fee 97
file 16
financial 92
firm (n) 43
flash (n) 20
float 21
form (n) 15
frank 89
frightening 24

generous 78
get along with 97
get rid of 105
give someone a hand 78
go off (ring) 61

honest 78
housework 3

imaginary 8
impress 79
inaccurate 71
include 60
increase (v) 6
informative 97
injured 44
inn 102
insect 28
install 105
instruct 92
introduce 1
invention 46
jam (n) (food) 106
traffic jam 102
jewellery 34
join in 97
journalist 17

keep on 97
keep fit 102
kennel 103
knock down 105

ladder 24
lazy 69
lay (egg) 2
leisure 3
level (n) 92
library 97

licence 38
lift (n) (in a car) 54
live (adj) 91
live on 97
lively 89
look forward to 61
look up 6
luggage 57

maid 60
manage 15
map 39
mean (adj) 78
mind (n) 16
mind (v) 12
minimum 15
miss (a bus) 51
miss (a person) 70
misunderstand 52
monster 60
motorway 101
move house 2
muddy 43
murder (n, v) 71

nail (of finger) 80
neighbour 79
nervous 7
newsagent's 28
nightmare 42
notice (v) 25

octopus 42
offer 30
old-fashioned 69
order (n) 12
organise 11
outbreak 97
outcome 44
owe 33
on your own 12

pack (v) 105
package holiday 60
park (v) 20
pass out 61
patient (adj) 89
pavement 45
pedestrian 37
permission 15
permitted 15
personally 61
persuade 91

84

pet 1	receive 73	shake hands 2	tent 33
pick up (lift) 61	receptionist 60	shelf 106	thoughtful 89
pillow 106	record (v) 96	show up 21	tie (n) 15
play (n) 2	regret (v) 61	shower 24	tight 30
play (part of) 96	rehearsal 92	shy 78	till (n) 17
point (there's no) 61	reliable 78	single 47	tiring 10
polite 15	remain 79	slave 66	tolerant 89
pollution 48	removal 105	snack 16	torch 44
population 6	request (n) 16	snake 78	towel 106
possessions 15	require 15	solve 102	traditional 60
post (v) 6	rest (n) 60	sort out 11	transport 3
prediction 47	revise 6	souvenir 20	trainee 17
prevent 96	ring up 61	spare time 98	try on 30
produce (v) 6	romantic 89	staff 15	turn up 61
progress (n) 52	routine 2	stare 21	type (v) 12
properly 60	rubbish 60	stool 106	
prospects 17	rude 15	store (shop) 29	unexpectedly 24
punctual 15	run out 28	strap 29	upset (v) 69
punishment 8		stretch (v) 43	
purchase 96	salary 15	strict 64	van 105
purse 25	satellite 97	stripes 34	variety 17
put on weight 51	scared 79	stuffed 61	
	scenery (theatre) 92	supposed 105	wardrobe 106
quality 29	scream (n, v) 24		waste (v) 52
queue (v) 60	search (v) 25	take a decision 12	weapon 6
	selfish 78	take a photo 61	weigh 2
radiator 105	send for 97	take notes 17	weight 51
rainbow 42	serve 6	take part in 97	well-paid 17
rate 60	set off 97	talkative 88	whistle 2
realise 25	settee 106	tempered, bad 78	widely 3

Workbook Answers

Unit 1

1   Possible answers:
    a   and make my own breakfast.
    b   or sometimes I have a bath.
    c   I leave and walk to the bus-stop.
    d   for at least ten minutes.
    e   by 8.30 if I'm lucky.
    f   but it doesn't happen often.
    g   and I go home straight away.
    h   but usually I stay at home.

3   Suggested answers:
    a   When did you leave school?
    b   What did you do then?
    c   How long did you work as a trainee manager?
    d   Why did you leave?
    e   What do you do now?

4   1 choose   2 decide/find/realise   3 don't enjoy/like
    4 became   5 knew   6 like/love   7 thought
    8 told   9 decided/found/realised   10 wanted
    11 decided   12 works
    13 enjoy/love/like   14 meet   15 changes

5   go skating, go shopping, go swimming, go jogging, go camping, go sailing

6   possible   adjective
    possibly   adverb
    possibility   noun
    impossible   adjective
    advice   noun
    advise   verb
    adviser   noun
    advisable   adjective
    encourage   verb
    encouragement   noun
    encouraged   adjective
    discourage   verb
    imagine   verb
    imagination   noun
    imaginary   adjective
    imaginative   adjective

7   a advice   b possibility   c imagination
    d discouraged   e advice/encouragement
    f impossible   g advises   h imaginative

8   make: a joke, an offer, a noise, a choice, a cake, a mistake, a decision
    do: business, some homework, some housework, an exercise, the shopping

9   b   1 wear   2 dress   3 dresses   4 put on   5 wears

11 b   fit   hate   bore   hair   beat
    c   **Louise**   We also **had to** wear school uniform, we had to wear a brown **skirt** and a beige jumper and a cream **shirt** with a brown **tie**. And it wasn't a very comfortable uniform to wear and it wasn't very **attractive** either, but we had to wear it, it was very strictly enforced. And they **always** made sure that we had **our hair** cut neatly and we didn't wear make-up or **earrings**.

Unit 2

1   1 work   2 makes   3 don't like   4 do   5 want   6 tells
    7 is looking   8 are building   9 doesn't dress
    10 arrives   11 is training   12 goes   13 don't send
    14 comes   15 am writing,   16 is cooking

2   a 5   b 4   c 7   d 6   e 3   f 1   g 2

3   Suggested answers:
    vet – *animals*   teacher – *pupils*
    accountant – *money*   bank clerk – *cheques*
    mechanic – *cars*   shop assistant – *customers*
    nurse – *patients*   waiter – *tips*
    architect – *buildings*   photographer – *models*
    surgeon – *operations*   plumber – *pipes*
    lawyer – *courts*   dustman – *rubbish*
    actor – *audiences*

4   b dustman   c mechanic   d photographer
    e plumber   f nurse   g waiter   h accountant

5   1 training   2 involve   3 staff   4 deal   5 polite
    6 employer   7 punctual   8 paid

6   a   welcome the guests and make them feel at home, answer their enquiries and give them information
    b   show them to their rooms
    c   it is interesting, working nights, customers are rude
    d   polite
    e   to do a training course
    f   become a hotel manager, have my own hotel

7 | Noun | Adjective |
    | --- | --- |
    | experience | experienced |
    | enthusiasm | enthusiastic |
    | versatility | versatile |
    | confidence | confident |
    | responsibility | responsible |

Noun	Adjective
organisation	organised
reliability	reliable
patience	patient
honesty	honest
independence	independent

8   a enthusiasm   b honest   c independent
    d organised   e confidence   f versatile
    g reliable   h patience

10 b   At the moment Nancy Hills works as the assistant manager in a large department store in the centre of Bradford.
    c   She started working there in 1989.
    d   Before that, she worked as a typist.

4 a I think it might snow tomorrow.
  b There is a pub on the corner of this street.
  c It is a small but interesting town.
  d There is no point in waiting all afternoon.
  e It isn't far to the post office from here.
  f There is a lot of work for us to do.
  g It is very warm today.
  h Is there time for a drink?

5 a He was so tired (that) he went home to bed.
  b It was such a sunny day (that) we decided to go for a swim.
  c She ate so much (that) she began to feel ill.
  d She ate such a lot (that) she began to feel ill.
  e I haven't had such a good time for ages.
  f It was such a heavy case (that) I couldn't lift it.

6 a You are not old enough/are too young to see this film.
  b It's not warm enough/too cold to go swimming today.
  c I'm not tall enough/too short to reach that shelf.
  d This piece of string is not long enough/is too short.
  e This tea is too hot to drink.
  f You're too late, the lesson has started.

7 a look forward to b put me c break down d try on
  e give up f pick up g deal with h pass out i get on with j turn up k pick someone up l look up
  m run out of

8 a put me up b get on with them c broke down
  d have run out of e look forward to f deal with
  g picked them up h turned up i pick you up
  j tried it on

10 b 1 attraction 2 formerly 3 reconstructed
  4 restored 5 damaged 6 site 7 excavation
  8 preserved

11 b I remembered there was a very nice campsite just outside Paris which I visited with my family as a child. So I decided that I would book that in advance because it was high season, middle of August, um and **I'm very glad I did** because we were really very squashed into this campsite. Um the **problem with it obviously**, is that you don't have the luxuries that you would have in a hotel. The facilities were fairly good but the showers **never really were very hot** even though they claimed in the brochure that they would be hot, they weren't really, um . . . and you have to wait for your shower and if you need the toilet in the night **you have to walk half a mile** across the campsite to the nearest wash area. But we were right, our tent was right next to the river which was very nice except for the mosquitoes, the mosquitoes were huge.

Unit 8

1 **Positive:** easygoing, responsible, understanding, careful
   strict could be positive, depending on the user's attitude.
  Negative: lonely, strict, unreliable, lazy, shy, worried, bored.

2 a bored b shy c easygoing d lonely e lazy
  f unreliable g strict h worried

3 a Liz told John not to wait for her because she wouldn't be back until eight.
  b 'Well, everybody, you have done/you did very well in the test.'
  c Lucy told Joe that she was leaving at six after she had finished the painting.
  d 'Robert, when I see you I'll tell you the news.'
  e Michael told Jane that he couldn't talk for long because he was cooking the dinner.
  f 'This dog of mine has been chasing the neighbour's cat.'
  g Sarah explained to Bill that she had been too tired to go out.
  h Ann told us that after she had finished school she was going to travel round the world.

4 a you, tomorrow b it, the c it, then d her, last night e the books, that afternoon f there, the day before

5 a Kate asked John to put it on the desk.
  b Brian told Sue that he would see her there the following day.
  c She said that she had taken it to the cleaner's the week before.
  d Jim said that she was joining him there the following year.
  e Paul told Mary that the last thing he wanted was to leave her there.
  f Graham said that he had left it on the table the day before.

6 Suggested answers:

  Meetings with ministers
  The spokesman said that ministers would meet in a week's time to make decisions, but the Prime Minister said that they would make their decisions on the following day.

  Decisions about pay rises
  The spokesman said that ministers had agreed to stop all pay rises for government employees, but the Prime Minister said that there had been no discussion about this.

  Income tax
  The spokesman said that the Prime Minister wanted to increase income tax, but the Prime Minister said that there would definitely not be a rise.

Interviewer: So you wouldn't consider running even a small car?
Lynn: **It doesn't make any sense** for me. The big problem is parking – there's simply nowhere to put it **if you drive into** the centre, unless you feel like paying a fortune in a car park.

Unit 6

1 a an, a, the   b –,–,–   c the,–,–   d –,–   e –,–,–
   f –, the, –,   g to, the, the   h a, the

2 a is having   b will be   c will be living   d are going to drop   e I am flying   f will,   g will we use   h I'll take

3 a starts, will take   b comes, will tell
   c will wait, phones   d leaves, will give
   e can, come   f will pay, get

4 a Sorry, but you have too much luggage.
   b Sorry, but I haven't got enough money.
   c Oh dear, we haven't got enough furniture.
   d The trouble is nowadays that there is too much fighting at football matches.
   e That's a bit better. But you still haven't done enough work.

5 a it is   b is   c is   d was   e is   f was

6 a some   b some   c some   d a   e a   f a   g some
   h some

7 a We won't be there at six if the train is late.
   b If you don't go away, I'll call the police.
   c You won't pass the exam if you do something silly.
   d If you don't take more exercise, you won't start feeling better.
   e You won't catch the bus if you don't leave now.
   f If you don't pay for my ticket. I'm not coming.

8 a makes   b make   c having   d take   e taking
   f make

9 1 first of all   2 as well as this   3 for example
   4 besides   5 however   6 although   7 on the other hand   8 finally

11 b 1 call   2 dialled   3 got through   4 range off
      5 operator   6 telephone directory

12 b I don't think we'll have cars any more, they just **waste too much energy** and make a lot of noise and pollution and all that. So I should think **we'll all be using** some kind of public system, but not buses like we've got now. Maybe some kind of electric railway, either underground or maybe **high over the city**. Everything will be electric, but I think the power will come from the sun, or maybe even from the wind, because there won't be **any coal or oil left**. I don't think things will be **much different really**. I expect we'll all be sitting at home and watching some kind of super satellite TV. I don't think I'm **looking forward to it** really. There'll be computers everywhere and life will be all about pushing buttons.

Progress Test 2 Units 3, 4, 5 and 6

1 a left, haven't done   b have you seen, put   c bought, have just had   d did you stay, did you enjoy
   e haven't been, saw   f have broken   g wrote
   h visited   i didn't realise, have you known
   (15 marks)

2 a went, was boiling, rang   b was waiting, met, had
   c stayed, went, drew   d did you do, happened, ran, called   e rang, was having
   (15 marks)

3 a Your house is larger than mine.
   b This restaurant is the most expensive.
   c The last film was not as good as this one.
   d Jim was the worst player on the field.
   e The first question was more difficult than/not as easy as the second one.
   (5 marks)

4 a the, the, the   b –, an   c a, –   d –, –   e –, the, the
   f the, a   g a, a/the   h the, –
   (9 marks)

5 Suggested answers:
   a Shall I carry it for you?
   b If it is bad, we'll stay at home.
   c I expect I'll be famous.
   d No, I have been here before.
   e Sorry, I was doing my homework.
   (5 marks)

6 a enough   b some, too   c too   d many, enough
   e much, little   f some, much   g some, enough
   (6 marks)

Unit 7

1 a That can't be John's bike.
   b I might see you again next week.
   c You must know what I mean.
   d It could break, you know.
   e I might not go to Japan this summer.
   f This must be the Tower of London.

2 a You had better go home now.
   b This must be the place where I lost my wallet.
   c Do you have to go shopping again?
   d You must stop smoking.
   e You have to go back to the first square.
   f He doesn't have to work on Saturdays.

3 a Peter saved all his pocket money to buy a new motorbike.
   b Sue turned down the television so that Jack could use the phone.
   c Jim covered his face so that people couldn't recognise him.
   d Bill picked up the dictionary to look up a word.
   e Julie went into the bathroom to have a shower.
   f Martin lit some candles so that people could see in the dark.

89

Ann: Roger, **of course not**. You know you can trust me, don't you? Now, just listen carefully and I'll **go over** the directions again.

c Assistant: This is our most **popular model**. It's light, very strong, and completely safe.
Ricky: I had **one of those**, and I didn't think it was very safe. I burnt myself once.
Jean: **Isn't the gas one safer?**
Assistant: Some people prefer gas. But the advantage with this one is that you can **light it much more easily** in a strong wind, or if it's raining.

Unit 4

1 a Are you doing?   b is going to crash   c going to sleep   d starts   e will win   f what are you going to give   g I am meeting   h will be leaving

2 Suggested answers:
 a Where are you going (to go) on holiday this year?
 b What are you doing this evening?
 c What time does the plane leave?
 d What are you going to do when you leave school?
 e Why are you taking the bus?

3 a from, to , in   b in, on   c at, in   d on/at, opposite   e on, at   f to, on, at   g by, at/in   h in

5 Suggested answer:
 – Excuse me, how much is this dress?
 – Which one is the best?
 – Have you got a larger size?
 – I am going home to Italy tomorrow.
 – How about this one?
 – Can I try it on?

5 Suggested answers:
 a I'll take the blue one.
 b Why don't you buy her a diary?
 c Shall I make you a sandwich?
 d I'm visiting my grandmother on Sunday.
 e Do you think you could open the window?

6 Suggested answers:
 a Fresh vegetables are tastier than frozen vegetables.
 b Meat is more expensive than fish.
 c Tinned milk is more convenient than fresh milk.
 d Fresh food is healthier than frozen food.
 e Fast food is more fattening than health food.
 f Home-grown fruit is better than imported fruit.

7 1 happened 2 went 3 decided 4 found 5 need 6 take 7 know 8 miss 9 keeps 10 phoned 11 was 12 told 13 coming 14 understand/know 15 will call

8 Vegetables: cabbage, onions, carrots, beans
 Fruit: apples, grapes, peaches, pears
 Dairy: yoghurt, cheese, milk, cream
 Meat: chops, sausages, steak, chicken
 Bakery: bread, biscuits, cakes, rolls

11 b 1 Small corner shops are much more expensive than supermarkets.
 2 What are you doing tonight after the lesson?
 3 Excuse me, do you know the way to the bus station?
 4 I'm looking for a pub called 'The Coach and Horses'.
 5 I'll come round and pick you up at half past seven.

Unit 5

1 a for   b ago   c already   d before   e lately   f yet   g a moment ago   h ever

2 1 for many years/for ages 2 recently 3 two weeks ago 4 since 5 when 6 ago 7 when 8 since 9 for ages 10 very often

3 a did he go   b have you known   c haven't driven   d haven't been   e asked, refused   f started   g has never had   h did you do, broke down

4 1 directions 2 turn 3 to 4 take 5 brings 6 junction 7 straight 8 on 9 opposite 10 at

6 Suggested answers:
 a I've been studying for my exams.
 b No thanks, I've had lunch already.
 c Yes, I went there in 1989.
 d Sorry, I haven't finished it yet.
 e Yes, I met him at a party last year.
 f Yes, I've known him since we were at school together.
 g I've just had a bath.
 h Sorry, he's just left.

7 1 was cycling 2 had 3 was raining 4 slipped 5 fell 6 stopped 7 Have you hurt 8 have broken 9 don't worry 10 I'll take 11 gave 12 asked 13 have you eaten 14 what do you mean 15 did you have 16 left 17 Am I going to have 18 I have just made

8 b Recently I bought a **brand new** car. It was in a lovely condition and very **luxurious**. People told me I would **save** a lot of money **on** petrol and they were **impressed**. I showed it to a friend of mine who is a mechanic. He disagreed. '**It's not worth much**,' he said. 'Why don't you let me put in a new engine? I felt very confused!

9 b **Lynn:** I would say it cost me about £5 or £6 a week. Sometimes I get a Travelcard, which you can use on the tube or on the buses, and **sometimes I get** the bus. It depends how organised I'm feeling that week. **It's very easy** to use public transport, it's much cheaper than a car, and there's **lots of it**, you can get anywhere quickly, especially on the Underground. While in a car you get stuck in a traffic jam.

e   Now she works in the toy department but last year she worked in the children's clothes department.
f   She has to serve customers but she is also learning to be a manager.
g   Last month she went to London to do a training course and learn to use a computer.
h   She did not like being a typist because there was no responsibility.

11 b   1   What do you do for a living?
        2   This sounds like a good job.
        3   She has painted a lot of portraits.
        4   Do you do all your own hair?
        5   I met her by accident.
        6   I don't like the way he gossips.
        7   I planned to go out yesterday but I stayed in instead.
        8   I'm looking forward to my holiday in the summer.
        9   Don't forget to get in touch with the personnel manager.
        10 What sort of job do you want?

12 b   Interviewer: And do you do the same things all the time?
        Janet: **At the moment**, yes I do, it's very much the same things all the time, but we change around, and I could go to a different department soon **for example**. It **all depends**.
        Interviewer: What about the daily routine? Do you have one?
        Janet: Oh yes, **definitely**. The main thing I do first is, I check the till.
        Interviewer: That's the drawer with the money in it.
        Janet: Yes, **that's right**.

Progress Test 1   Units 1 and 2

1   a 3   b 1   c 4   d 2   e 3   f 4   g 2   h 3   i 4   j 1
                                                              (10 marks)

2   a did you eat, Did you go   b do you do   c fell, had   d don't want, is raining   e Does Sue like   f do you usually stay, go   g Do you usually understand, tells   h did you do   i was, is talking
                                                              (15 marks)

3   a   Does Philip work in an electronics factory?
    b   Did they have to write their homework again?
    c   Does Julie often have to work at weekends?
    d   Is Richard waiting for us downstairs?
    e   Did they lose their suitcases at the airport?
    f   Are you reading my newspaper?
    g   Does Janet like fish and chips?
    h   Did Helen know all the answers?
    i   Do they usually stay at the Grand Hotel?
    j   Did Sally leave this morning?
                                                              (5 marks)

4   Suggested answers:
    1 left   2 job   3 had/used   4 every   5 same   6 first   7 deal   8 take   9 paid   10 spends
                                                              (10 marks)

Unit 3

1   a was, making, heard   b put on, went   c was looking for, wanted   d explained, was having   e forgot, was still cooking   f burnt   g opened, saw   h was sitting, was trying   i put, left   j smelt jumped

2   1 happened   2 was travelling   3 was sitting   4 realised   5 didn't have   6 got out   7 took   8 didn't find   9 went   10 bought   11 arrived   12 contained   13 made   14 was putting   15 noticed   16 didn't know

3   Suggested answers:
    b then   c in the end   d when   e while   f when

5   a 4   b 8   c 3   d 2   e 1   f 7   g 6   h 5

6   Suggested answers:
    a   What did you do when you found it?
    b   And what were you doing in Mr Smythe's bedroom?
    c   And when do you usually clean the house?
    d   Why did you come on Wednesday/ Why were you cleaning it on Wednesday?
    e   Why did he ask you to come on Wednesday?

7   Suggested answers:
    a   meeting interesting people
    b   to try something different
    c   to travel more
    d   working at night
    e   to deal with angry customers
    f   making everything sound interesting
    g   sitting indoors all the time
    h   try to enjoy it

8   a to   b at, at   c on, on   d from, at   e in/at, out of   f into, at, at   g from, to   h on, in

9   a you go, turn   d shall I give you
    b shall I help   e I'll cook the lunch
    c feed the dog   f could I borrow

10 b   1   make a trip   5   protected
        2   turned into   6   rescue
        3   ran out of   7   raised the alarm
        4   waved   8   landed

11 b   back   thin   win   lock   fan   those   shock   rise
    c   Roger: Got it. But just remind me again who I'm going to see.
        Ann: **Ask for** Mr Stubbs. His office is on the second floor. Give him the packet and he'll give you an envelope in exchange. **It's quite simple**. Then you bring the envelope back here.
        Roger: Are you sure this is all right Ann? There's nothing, **you know**, wrong about all this, **is there**. It does seem a bit fishy to me.

Decisions about prices
The spokesman said that the price of cigarettes would rise, but the Prime Minister said there would be no increase.

Old age pensions
The spokesman said that the old age pension would go up by 10% after Christmas, but the Prime Minister said that it would go up 15% before Christmas.

7 b 1 My boss annoyed me so much that I lost my temper.
    2 Jack is a very helpful boy and his manners are excellent.
    3 Mandy and Paul have decided not to get married because they have nothing in common.
    4 When nobody writes to me it gets me down.
    5 Brenda is very good at handling emergencies.
    6 Martin confessed to Sue that he had been telling lies about her.
    7 Katherine and Diane have always looked up to their father.
    8 Derek doesn't get on with his sister.

8 b I found that hard to believe, and later I talked to the boys' mother. I told her what her husband **had said**, and she burst out laughing. When I asked her why, she told me that her sons had done **all kinds of things** that their father knew nothing about. I asked her for some examples, and it turned out that the boys had done **quite a lot of** smoking and drinking in secret, both at home, and when out with their friends. But she said that she hadn't been angry with them when she found out. She hadn't forgotten **what it was like** to be a teenager, and remembered getting into trouble herself, and being locked in her room. She said she had decided when she had children that she wouldn't **make the same mistakes** her parents had made.

Unit 9

1 Suggested answers:
  a If you stand up, the boat will sink.
  b If it rains, we'll go to the cinema.
  c If you aren't careful, you'll drop it.
  d If my boss catches me, he'll be very angry.
  e If you don't send it express, it won't arrive in time.
  f If you give up sweets, you'll lose some weight.
  g You won't feel cold if you wear this.
  h If you lend me some money, I'll pay you back next week.

2 a 4 b 8 c 1 d 5 e 2 f 7 g 3 h 6

3 a honest b shy c generous d aggressive e selfish f rude g brave h confident i reliable j mean

4 Suggested answers:
  a If I were you, I'd buy the green one.
  b I think you should take the 2.00.
  c Why don't you take an asprin.
  d I wouldn't do that, if I were you.
  e I don't think that's a very good idea.
  f I'd take a holiday, if I were you.
  g I think you should call a plumber.
  h Why don't you complain to the manager.

5 a I could post my letter if I had a stamp.
  b If you fall in, the life-guard will rescue you.
  c If I knew the answer I would tell you.
  d If I were a farmer, I would feel lonely.
  e We won't leave tomorrow if there is a change in the weather.

8 b 1 sympathetic 2 self-conscious 3 direct 4 nervous 5 lively 6 caring 7 realistic 8 embarrassed.

9 a import**a**nt **v**it**a**l commu**ni**cati**o**n nerv**ou**s post**u**re **o**bserve suffer**e**r neg**a**tive

  b import<u>a</u>nt <u>v</u>ital commu<u>ni</u>cation <u>n</u>ervous <u>p</u>osture ob<u>s</u>erve <u>s</u>ufferer <u>n</u>egative

  c **Interviewer:** David, you were **in trouble a lot** when you were young, weren't you.
    David: Yes I'm afraid I was **the sort of kid** who was always fighting and causing trouble at school. It was just the way I grew up, and I didn't really see it as a problem. I was always very noisy, both **at home and at** school. My mother didn't let me in the house a lot of the time, and of course I was always **in hot water at** school with the teachers. I guess I was just very aggressive, you know, always looking for trouble. I remember **one of my teachers** telling me that every time I opened my mouth **I put my foot in it.**

Unit 10

1 a worried b frank c bored d tolerant e cheerful f suspicious g determined h lively i jealous j patient

2
Adjective	Noun
determined	determination
jealous	jealousy
suspicious	suspicion
tolerant	tolerance
frank	frankness
patient	patience
bored	boredom
worried	worry

3 a worries b suspicion c boredom d frankness e patience f determination g tolerance h jealousy

4 1 what 2 how 3 who 4 what 5 what 6 where 7 who 8 how 9 who 10 what

5 Circled <u>who</u> in sentences: **a, e, h,**

6 Suggested answers:
  a I'm having a party on Saturday. Would you like to come?

91

b Would you like a cup of tea?
c If I were you, I'd give up smoking.
d How about going to the cinema?
e Hello. I'm Michael.

7 a Joe asked Sue where she was going.
b Peter asked them if they had seen the new film on at the Odeon.
c Frances asked Nick why he hadn't told her before.
d Paula asked him if she had left her gloves there the night before.
e Keith asked Jill if she was going home when the lesson finished.
f Sheila's mother asked her who usually sat next to her in English.
g Michael asked Judith if she was going to be there the following year.
h Charlie's sister asked him why he was crying.

8 a give/lend b put c driving d crashed e passed f change g give h is

9 Suggested answers:
1 best 2 other 3 since 4 with 5 clothes 6 what 7 good 8 both 9 spend 10 is/seems

11 b 1 on and off 2 insisted on 3 single 4 join 5 took place 6 cruel 7 date 8 give up

12 b I've got a neighbour who I suppose is one of my best friends, and I think I admire her most because she says **exactly what she thinks**. I'm sure she would never lie to me. Even little things, like if I say **'Does this hairstyle suit me?'** she'll tell me exactly what she thinks. I think that friends have **to tell you the truth**, don't you? She's also the kind of person I can always depend on if I need anything – you know, **I can leave the children with her**, or I can borrow some sugar, and I know she won't complain about it. **And I do the same for her.**

Progress Test 3   Units 7, 8, 9, and 10

1 a Carol asked John if he wanted coffee.
b The teacher told the girls not to leave their bags near the door.
c Alice told Mary that she would help her if she had time.
d Alan said that he had left the money on top of the fridge.
e Sheila told Harry she was taking the 4.30 train.
f Patsy asked Dave when the film started.
g Brian asked Valerie if she had been there on Wednesday.
h Paul asked Jack if he could borrow his radio.
i Nigel asked me if my dog had had any puppies.
j Helen told the teacher she had forgotten her homework.

(10 marks)

2 a It can't be Tuesday today.
b We don't have to wear school uniform in this school.
c I think you had better stay in bed for a couple of days.
d We might miss the bus.
e That must be John over there.

(10 marks)

3 a too, to b not, enough c so, could d too, to
e such, enough f to, too g too, to h enough, to
i too, to j so, could

4 a had, would buy b hear, will let c keep, will lose
d were, wouldn't spend e will give, get f stand, will fall g wouldn't feel, didn't smoke h will wait, come
i don't stop, will call j used, wouldn't be

(10 marks)

5 1 whether 2 there 3 enough 4 are 5 spend
6 forward 7 all 8 in 9 than 10 so

(10 marks)

Unit 11

1 a These biscuits are made in our Bristol factory.
b All the money was taken from the cashier's desk.
c It has been decided to close the office on Thursday.
d At the meeting a speech will be given by Mr Johnson.
e Janet is being met at the airport.
f Nothing is known about the missing jewellery.
g A cheque is usually signed with a pen, not a pencil.
h She was recorded singing live at a night-club.

2 a Someone has cut down my cherry tree.
b They make these pullovers in Scotland.
c A man in a fishing boat rescued them.
d They did not help her at the police station.
e All of us will remember this trip.
f They are selling their house.
g Harold Pinter wrote this play.
h Her brother did not take her advice.

3 a Our Christmas party has to be organised.
b The guests should be invited this week.
c Some of them will have to be telephoned.
d All the food has to be bought.
e The decorations have to be put up.
f The presents have to be wrapped.
g A baby-sitter has to be found.
h The turkey has to be cooked for a long time.

4 Suggested answers:
better   less expensive   more convenient
more exciting   exciting   more sociable   easier
better   more relaxing   more interesting

5 a for b to c for d on e of f in g off h in

6 a I decided to look up the word in the dictionary.
b I asked if I could try on the trousers to see if they fitted.
c I couldn't make the cake because we ran out of flour.
d I get on well with my mother-in-law.
e If you like, we could put you up.
f Halfway up the hill the bus broke down.

g You'll never guess who turned up at the party last night!
h Could you pick me up at about 9.30?

8 b 1 quickly 2 equally 3 finally 4 eagerly
       5 clearly 6 vaguely

   c | Noun | Adjective | Noun | Verb |
      |---|---|---|---|
      | perfection | perfect | narration | narrate |
      | exhaustion | exhausted | destruction | destroy |
      | privacy | private | contribution | contribute |

9 b Jenny: I talked to some cinema-goers waiting outside a cinema in London. **How did they feel** about Freddy?
      Girl: A bit stupid I think, OK for young kids, but **I don't go in for** that kind of film myself. I might watch one if I was really bored I suppose.
      Boy: I like the violence, I mean it's done well in the films, and the make-up and the effects **are really good**. And actually they're very funny films. **Good for a laugh.**
      Woman: Oh no, I wouldn't let my children watch films like that, it gives them nightmares for a start, and they don't really understand **that it isn't real**. I don't expect they even know that it's an actor who plays Freddy.

Unit 12

1 a I'd rather go to bed than stay up late.
   b I prefer to live in the town centre.
   c I'd rather live in a flat than a house.
   d He would rather drink coffee than tea.
   e We would rather go by train.
   f I prefer to travel by bus.
   g Would you like to sleep in this room?
   h I would rather leave now.

2 a The council says that our town is going to be improved.
   b Last year a new library was built in the city centre.
   c And recently a lot of trees have been planted.
   d And the swimming pool is being improved.
   e Last year a lot of damage was done by hooligans.
   f Slogans were painted on the walls outside.
   g And all the windows were broken.
   h Now all the damage is going to be repaired.

3 1 was owned   2 was not lived in   3 have been painted
   4 has been reorganised   5 was cut off   6 be done
   7 was paid   8 is going to be knocked down
   9 is going to be made   10 have been visited
   11 have not been invited back   12 was being done

4 a More blocks of flats should be built in this city.
   b I think this road should be widened.
   c Traffic should be banned from the city centre.
   d Something could be done about the noise.
   e More trees and bushes should be planted here.
   f All those ugly buildings could be knocked down.
   g The old buildings should be restored.
   h The plans for the new motorway could be changed.

5 Suggested answers:
   a I think it should be knocked down.
   b I'd rather live in a large flat because I would like to live in the city centre.
   c There used to be more small houses with gardens.
   d The bathroom hasn't been painted yet.
   e More trees could be planted, and some parks could be made.

6 c is nearest to the school
   b and c might be noisy
   a offers the best facilities
   a – would be difficult to travel to school and expensive
   b – could be noisy and might need more furniture
   c – could be noisy, outside bathroom, bad condition
   d – no public transport to the centre and quite expensive

8 a | Verb | Noun | Adjective |
      |---|---|---|
      | construct | construction | constructed |
      | restore | restoration | restored |
      | modernise | modernisation | modernised |
      | carpet | carpet | carpeted |
      | convert | conversion | converted |

   b 1 central heating 2 mobile home 3 ceiling
      4 view 5 space 6 around 7 shower 8 bargain

9 b Our house as you can see is completely underground, not because **we wanted it this way**, but when we bought this land and decided to build a house, the local council wouldn't let us put up a proper one because it would spoil the view. Yes, I found it **hard to believe too**. Anyway, we decided that we wouldn't be beaten by them, and so we had plans made for this house. You can't see **much of it from the outside**. Down under here the house is actually quite large. It's very warm of course, and we get some light from the roof windows, but mainly we have electric lights. It's got three bedrooms, a kitchen and a living room. I must admit **it did take me a while** to get used to it, but now I think it's a really nice house. We go upstairs to the garden in our house . . .

Final test

1 a offered b am staying c arrives d have you seen
   e did you do f were, would try g have you been studying h have never seen i do j was going
   k was having l has just been stolen m do you do
   n did you arrive o is

                                                    (15 marks)

2 Suggested answers:
   a I don't think I would buy a new car if I were you.
   b I'm sorry I'm late, but I missed the bus.
   c Could I leave early please?

  d I think I'll take this black pair.
  e Why don't we go to the zoo tomorrow?
  f That looks heavy. Shall I carry it for you?
  g Don't worry, I'll pay you back on Saturday.
  h Do you think you could you pass me the salt?
  i I'm playing tennis in the morning, and in the afternoon I'm going to do some studying.
  j I think that wider roads should be built.
                (10 marks)

3 **1** had **2** was working **3** got **4** told **5** had won
 6 decided **7** live **8** moved **9** have learned
 10 didn't have **11** lived **12** have also changed
 13 spend **14** have painted **15** am having **16** miss
 17 haven't been **18** think **19** would do **20** had
                (20 marks)

4 **a** John is a good driver.
 b Karen is much taller than Sue.
 c My hair is long.
 d You're not old enough to watch this film.
 e I think you had better take your raincoat with you.
 f You don't have to be here early.
 g This can't be the right station.
 h The windows have to be cleaned.
 i I've been reading this book for two hours.
 j Steve asked Elaine what she had done with his keys.
                (10 marks)

5 **a** for, for **b** ago, since **c** between, at **d** at, in
 e recently/lately, for **f** up, on **g** on, since
 h when, to **i** of, of **j** forward.
                (10 marks)